AUTOCAD LT
in easy steps

Paul Whelan

COMPUTER
STEP

In easy steps is an imprint of Computer Step
Southfield Road . Southam
Warwickshire CV33 OFB . England

Tel: 01926 817999 Fax: 01926 817005
http://www.computerstep.com

Reprinted 1999
First edition 1998

Notice of Liability

Every effort has been made to ensure that this book contains accurate
and current information. However, Computer Step and the author shall
not be liable for any loss or damage suffered by readers as a result of
any information contained herein.

Trademarks

AutoCAD LT® is a registered trademark of Autodesk Inc. All other
trademarks are acknowledged as belonging to their respective
companies.

Printed and bound in the United Kingdom

ISBN 1-84078-005-3

Contents

5   How to Edit Objects   55

6   Text, Points and Units   71

7   Working with Layers   83

8   Blocks and Xrefs   99

9   Dimensioning   125

Fundamental Concepts

In this chapter, you'll learn the difference between traditional draughting techniques and those used in AutoCAD LT. You will then start AutoCAD LT and become familiar with the Create New Drawing dialogue box. Setting the drawing units and the electronic paper size are concepts that must be understood before you draw; these are covered in detail. The layout of the AutoCAD LT screen is then described in conjunction with the different methods of giving the program commands. Lastly, emphasis is placed on the importance of the command line.

Covers

Chapter One

Traditional Draughting Techniques

Let us take a look at how you might set about drawing in the traditional way on paper. Before starting to draw, you decide on:

A scale of 1:1 means one unit on your drawing is the same as one unit in reality.

Scale
A drawing of an object that in reality is larger than your sheet of paper (such as an extension to a house) must be scaled down. Something that is too small to represent comfortably on paper (such as the face of a watch) must be scaled up.

Paper size
You must select the sheet of paper the drawing will fit on: eg, A4, A3, A2, etc.

Units
The units you use will depend on the conventions expected by the engineers, designers, or builders. You may for example work in the imperial or metric systems. Values may be so small that you have to use 'scientific' or exponential notation to dimension a drawing.

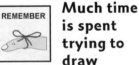

It's useful to know the size of sheets:

A4 = 297*210
A3 = 420*297
A2 = 594*420
A1 = 841*594
AO = 1189*841

Drawing instruments
Drawing tools such as a T-square, pens, erasers and ruler must be close at hand. Precision drawing tools are expensive and need to be maintained and replaced.

Drawing-board
A good board is essential to aid you in the accurate execution of the drawing.

Much time is spent trying to draw accurately with a pen. AutoCAD LT takes care of most of this for you if you learn to use the tools.

The drawing process
During a draughtperson's traditional training they learn to draw accurately the basic elements of a drawing: lines, arcs, circles, etc. Much time is spent selecting points accurately: the beginning and end points of lines, arcs, etc, and calculating distances.

Construction lines need to be drawn to locate points. Eventually, many of these construction lines will be erased.

AutoCAD LT Draughting Techniques

AutoCAD LT works in Real Size (1=1).

Scale

The problem of scaling is solved in a very dramatic way: there is NO scaling while producing your drawing in AutoCAD LT. All the dimensions you enter are input in real size (1=1). AutoCAD LT refers to this as inputting your drawing in Real World Co-ordinates. The computer will of course magnify the image to display it on the screen.

Paper size

When your drawing is completed you decide on the scale you want it printed on paper. A paper size is then selected which can accommodate the drawing.

If a table is 130cm by 75cm, you draw it 130*75cm in AutoCAD LT. Similarly, if a watch part has a 0.125mm diameter in reality, it is drawn 0.125 of a millimetre in AutoCAD LT.

Electronic paper size

While working in AutoCAD LT you draw in real world size, 1=1. This means that you must set up an electronic sheet of paper on the computer big enough to hold the drawing at 1=1.

For example, to set up an area on the computer screen to draw a ship of dimensions 210 metres by 32 metres you must tell AutoCAD LT that you need an electronic sheet at least 210 by 32 metres. You would probably set up a sheet of 250 by 50 metres. This will be enough space to accommodate the ship.

Units

This command allows you to set up the units you wish to work with.

Drawing instruments

AutoCAD LT provides 'tools' to help you draw accurately. For example, you can snap onto existing lines or circles.

Drawing board

This instrument has obviously been dispensed with.

If you want to draw a building, then the electronic sheet of paper must be a bit bigger than the building!

The drawing process

AutoCAD LT drawings are constructed from pre-defined entities or objects such as lines, arcs and circles. There is a command for each object type (eg, Line, Arc, Circle, etc.).

Starting and Finishing AutoCAD LT

Starting AutoCAD LT on...

There is a difference between 'Cancel' and 'OK' on the dialogue boxes: OK keeps the changes you made in the box.

- **Windows 95/98/NT and later versions**
  Click on the AutoCAD LT icon on the desktop. If no icon is present, click on 'Start' on the taskbar. Move the pointer to 'Programs'. Move the pointer to the AutoCAD LT folder and click on the AutoCAD LT icon.

- **On Windows 3.x**
  In the Program Manager you will see a group called AutoCAD LT. Double-click on it to open the group and then double-click on the AutoCAD LT icon. AutoCAD LT will then start. The 'Create New Drawing' dialogue box is then displayed.

Dialogue boxes

AutoCAD LT will display many dialogues boxes while you work. These dialogue boxes will:

- show the current setting the program is working with.

- allow you to change some of the settings if you wish.

The 'OK', 'Cancel', 'Close' and 'Done' buttons

If you do not save your work before you finish the program, it may ask you to 'Save changes to drawing'. The option Cancel will cancel the command to exit from AutoCAD LT.

If a dialogue box appears which you do not want then click on the 'Cancel' button.

If you change any settings in a dialogue box and you want AutoCAD LT to use the new settings then click on 'OK'.

'Done' is similar to 'OK'. Click on 'Done' when you have completed modifying the dialogue box.

'Close' will appear on some dialogue boxes. This is similar to 'Cancel'.

You may select the top right button icon 'x' to close the dialogue box without saving any changes.

Finishing AutoCAD LT

Save your work and then click on the 'x' button or under the File menu: File>Exit.

'Create New Drawing' Dialogue Box

This dialogue box sets up the electronic sheet size and the units for drawing. The AutoCAD LT 95, 97 and 98 dialogue box is shown below.

Users of LT previous to the 95, 97 and 98 releases will have a different dialogue box – see page 14.

Click one of these buttons to setup the electronic page

Opens an existing drawing

Tells you what each of the above buttons does

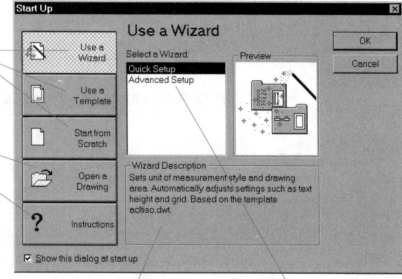

HANDY TIP

If you do not have the 'Create New Drawing' dialogue box on screen, select 'File' from the menu and click on 'New'.

Reminds you what the depressed button does

Contents change according to the button you select

Try clicking on each of the buttons to see the changes in the dialogue box.

What is a Wizard?

A 'wizard' will help you to carry out a task which you may not have had time to learn. There are two wizards here: Quick Setup and Advanced Setup.

Click on 'Use a Wizard'

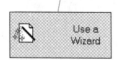

Click on the 'Use a wizard' button and then select the 'Quick Setup' wizard from the list by highlighting it.

Click on 'OK' to start the wizard.

The Drawing Units

The wizard proceeds to the 'Quick Setup' dialogue box. This dialogue box has two tabs: one for setting up the drawing units and the other to set the size of the electronic page on the computer.

Step 1: Units

AutoCAD LT wants to know what units you want to use while drawing. There are five fundamental types of units. Click on each of the units to see a sample.

1 unit = 1mm

Decimal refers to millimetres (mm).

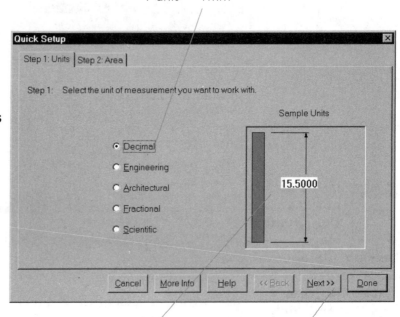

If you decide not to proceed with the setup, you must click 'Cancel'.

The number of decimal places can be set using the Units dialogue box

Do not click 'Done' until you have modified the tab 'Step 2 Area'

The units selected here will be used by AutoCAD LT for dimensioning the drawing. Also, input from the user will be accepted in these units only.

To proceed, select 'Decimal' and then click the 'Step 2: Area' tab.

The Electronic Paper Size

 REMEMBER

You cannot ignore a dialogue box. It demands a response from you. Clicking on any other part of the computer screen will not banish it. You must click 'Done' or 'Cancel'.

The size of the electronic sheet of paper must be large enough to contain the drawing in real size (1=1). If you are going to plot the finished drawing on standard paper sizes (A3, A2, A1, etc.), then it's a good idea to keep the proportions of the electronic sheet as a multiple of the standard paper sizes.

An example

Imagine the building you must draw is 30 by 20 metres. Convert this to mm by multiplying by 1000 (because you selected decimal (mm) as your unit in 'Step 1'). This is 30*1000 = 30,000mm; 20*1000 = 20,000mm. This building will fit on an A3 (420mm*297mm) sheet multiplied by 100 – ie, (420mm*297mm)*100 = 42,000*29,700. This is the electronic sheet size you want. It will hold the building in real size (1=1). You can later plot the work onto an A3 sheet by reducing the drawing by a factor of 100 (ie, plot at 1=100).

Step 2: Area

To tell AutoCAD LT that this is the electronic sheet size you want, enter 42,000 by 29,700 in the dialogue box (do not type in the thousand separator comma mark).

Double-click here. When the text is highlighted in blue, proceed to type in the electronic page size

Type 42000

Type 29700

Click 'Done' when you have finished

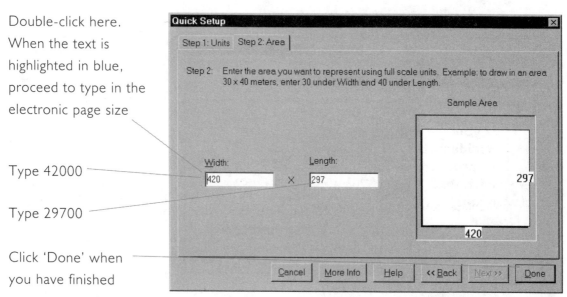

AutoCAD LT Release 2 Setup

 HANDY TIP

If you do not have the 'Create New Drawing' dialogue box on screen, select 'File' from the menu and click on 'New'.

The 'Create New Drawing' dialogue box for releases of AutoCAD LT previous to the 95, 97 and 98 editions is visually different, but it requires the same information: the drawing units and the electronic page size.

1 Select the 'Quick' method.

2 Make sure you have a tick here if you want this dialogue box to appear when you start AutoCAD LT the next time.

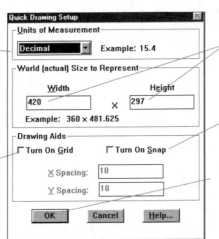

3 The prototype offered should be the *acltiso* file for the metric system.

4 Click 'OK' to proceed.

5 Make sure you have *Decimal* in here before you proceed. Click on the down arrow to see the available units.

6 Type 42000 and 29700 – see page 13 on how to calculate these values. Leave the snap blank for the moment.

7 If you tick here, a grid will appear on the drawing to show you the size of the electronic sheet.

8 Click 'OK' to proceed.

AutoCAD LT's Drawing Screen

AutoCAD LT releases previous to the 95, 97 and 98 editions may have different screens, but all the elements are still present.

The current drawing name. If this is 'Drawing.dwg' it means you have not given the drawing a name yet

The pull-down menus. These contain the drawing and editing commands

The Standard toolbar with frequently used commands

Object Properties toolbar

The 'Draw' toolbar

The 'Modify' toolbar

The drawing editor: this is where you draw. The grid of dots shows the size of the electronic sheet you setup

The 'Command line'. You can type commands here and watch for AutoCAD LT's response

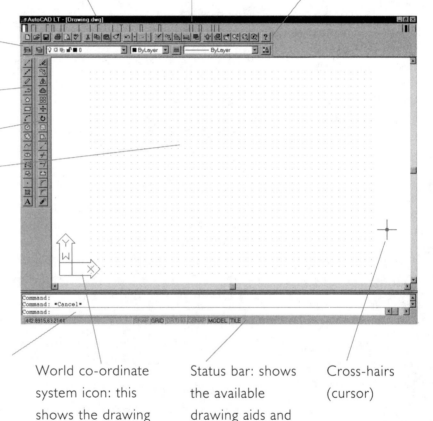

World co-ordinate system icon: this shows the drawing plane

Status bar: shows the available drawing aids and co-ordinates

Cross-hairs (cursor)

In some releases of AutoCAD LT the cross-hairs will be the width and height of the drawing editor and the world co-ordinate icon may not be visible. To make it visible issue the command UCSICON and use the option ON.

Giving Commands to AutoCAD LT

Pull-down menus

Just click on the menu name to see the list of commands. Click on a command to issue it. If a command has an arrow after it, a sub-menu will appear when you move the arrow cursor over it. Click on a command in the sub-menu to issue it. If a pull-down menu has three omission points after it then a dialogue box will appear when it is selected.

If you use a short-cut you do not need to pull down a menu. Ctrl+S will save the drawing.

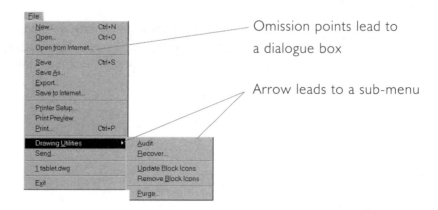

Omission points lead to a dialogue box

Arrow leads to a sub-menu

A menu produced as a result of a right-click of the mouse with the cursor over the drawing editor

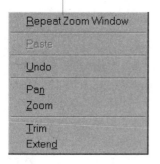

Using Alt+

The pull-down menus may also be selected by using 'Alt+ the underlined letter from the menu'. For example, hold down the Alt key and press the 'F' key to pull down the 'File' menu.

Shortcuts

For example Ctrl+S will issue the save command even if the pull down menu is not activated.

Right-clicking

Shortcut menus appear when you right-click the mouse (or pointing device). The short-cut menu will change as you right-click on different areas of the screen.

Try right-clicking over the drawing editor and then over the standard toolbar to see this context sensitive option in action.

...cont'd

Toolbars can be dragged out on to the drawing editor where they become floating toolbars. These floating toolbars can be moved around the screen.

You must keep your eye on the command line when drawing and editing. AutoCAD LT 'talks' to you there.

AutoCAD LT wants to know where the line is to start and end

AutoCAD LT is requesting the location of the centre point of the circle and its radius

Toolbar

Many commands can be issued by just clicking the appropriate icon from the toolbars.

Cursor menu

These menus are called up by using the shift key and a mouse button other than the 'click' (or left mouse) button:

If you have a two button mouse hold shift down and right-click.

If you have a three button mouse or an intellimouse use shift and the middle button or the wheel.

The Command line

The command line at the bottom of the drawing editor is very important in drawing with AutoCAD LT. You must keep checking what is written at this line as you draw and edit.

For example, if you draw a line AutoCAD LT will need to know where the line starts and ends. It will ask for these locations at the command line.

Again if you want to erase a line or a circle, AutoCAD LT will ask you which line or circle at the command line. The importance of the command line cannot be over emphasised.

Here are two examples of the command line requesting input from the user:

```
Command: 1
LINE From point:
To point:
0.8709<25                    SNAP GRID ORTHO OSNAP MODEL TILE
```

```
Command: c
CIRCLE 3P/2P/TTR/<Center point>: Diameter/<Radius>:
Command:
-2.5886,1.1716               SNAP GRID ORTHO OSNAP MODEL TILE
```

Saving a Drawing for the First Time

You could call up the 'Save As' dialogue box with the keystrokes Alt+F and then A. That is, hold down the Alt key and press F. This will drop-down the menu. Then press A for the underlined letter in 'Save As'.

A drawing which has no name will be titled **[Drawing]**. You should give the drawing a name as soon as you set it up. Don't wait until you have drawn some objects. All the settings such as the size of the drawing sheet and the units used are saved as part of the file.

Save and Save As

There are two ways to save the drawing. Both ways are found on the File drop-down menu. One is to use the 'Save' command and the other method is the 'Save As' command. Generally, 'Save As' is used if (1) you are saving a drawing for the first time (as in this case) and (2) if the drawing already has a name (other than 'Drawing') and you want to rename it as something else. Use 'Save' if the drawing already has a name.

1 Click on the drop-down menu 'File'.

2 Click on 'Save As'. The 'Save Drawing As' dialogue appears.

3 Type in a file name and click on 'Save'.

The drawing will be saved into the folder that is open here

Type the name in here. AutoCAD LT 95, 97 and 98 can take long file names; otherwise, keep the name to eight characters or less

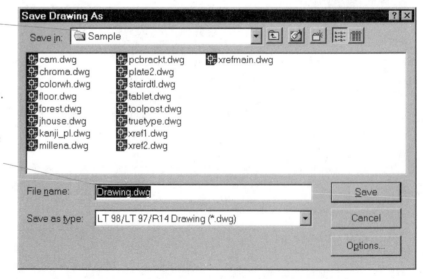

Basic Drawing Techniques

In this chapter, you'll learn the basic drawing techniques employed by AutoCAD LT. Great emphasis is placed on reading what is displayed at the command line. Recovering from errors in both your use of AutoCAD LT and in creating a drawing is outlined. The commands for drawing a circle and moving an entity are examined in detail. Mastering these commands is essential if you want to make progress in understanding what AutoCAD LT expects from you, the user. As a further aid to drawing accurately, we will look at the idea of snapping to an object using the end point of a line and the centre of a circle as examples. Finally, you will learn how to switch these object snap options on as background tools.

Chapter Two

Covers

Drawing a Line

HANDY TIP

Use the short-cut Ctrl+S to save the drawing regularly.

The command **LINE** (or simply **L** typed at the command line) will draw line entities in the drawing editor.

How the command works

When the command is executed, AutoCAD LT will ask you to specify the starting and end points of the line. Remember, you can use the command line, the drop-down menu or the toolbar. *Regardless of the method you use to give the command, you must look down at the command line to see how AutoCAD LT is responding.*

HANDY TIP

Instead of pressing Enter you could just press the spacebar.

Use one of these methods:

At the command line just type L and press Enter;

On the drop-down menu 'Draw,' click on Line, or;

On the toolbar click on the line icon.

REMEMBER

Keep your eye on the command line when you issue a command.

AutoCAD LT will ask 'From point:'. Click on a point and move the mouse. AutoCAD LT will now ask 'To point:'. Respond by clicking another point. AutoCAD LT will keep asking 'To point:' until you finish the command by pressing Enter.

Click on the first point in response to 'From point:'

AutoCAD LT will keep asking 'To point:' until you press Enter to terminate the command

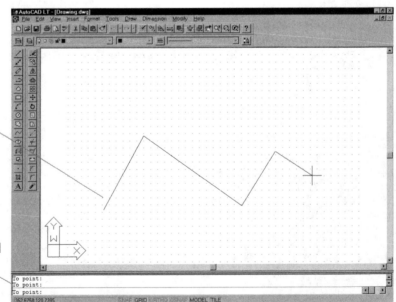

What to do if you Make a Mistake

Press Esc to cancel a command. When the command line is blank it is ready to accept another command. Users of AutoCAD Release 2 will need to press Ctrl + C to cancel.

Two types of mistakes frequently occur: mistakes associated with using AutoCAD LT itself and mistakes in the actual drawing you are working on.

Pressing the ESC key

The Esc key at the top left of the keyboard will get you out of most problems you encounter in using AutoCAD LT. Here are some examples of the times you would press the Esc key:

- If a command is not responding the way you expect
- If you want to cancel a command you started
- If you clicked a point on the screen unintentionally
- If a dialogue box appears on the screen accidentally

You may need to press Esc twice to cancel out of dimensioning, or if little blue boxes called grips appear in the drawing.

In all the cases above, pressing Esc once will free up the command line. When the command line is blank you can proceed to issue a new command. In some cases you may need to press the Esc key twice. For example, if you are dimensioning an entity and you decide you would like to return to a blank command line.

Using Undo

You can undo the last command by typing U at the command line and pressing the Enter key, or by clicking on the undo icon on the toolbar. You may undo several commands by clicking on the down arrow beside the Undo icon and selecting the actions you want undone by highlighting them.

All releases of AutoCAD LT previous to LT 98 allowed you to only redo the last command you applied Undo to.

Using Redo

The Redo command will reinstate the last command you applied undo to. You may redo several commands which were undone by clicking on the down arrow beside the Redo icon and selecting the actions you want to Redo by highlighting them.

Drawing a Circle

To draw a circle, use the following:

Command line: circle, or the alias 'c'

Menu: Draw>Circle

Toolbar:

How the command works

When the Circle command is issued AutoCAD LT will need to know where the centre of the circle is to be and its radius or diameter. The command line will prompt 'circle 3P/TTR/<Center point>:'. The text in angled brackets <> is the default option that AutoCAD LT offers. In other words if you click a point on the screen AutoCAD LT will accept that point as the centre of the circle. If you don't want to click the centre of the circle and instead use a different option, you must type the capitalised letter(s) of the option required. To draw a circle through three specified points you enter 3P at the command line and press the enter key. TTR must be typed to draw a circle with a radius that is a tangent to two objects.

Drawing with the Circle default options

In response to 'circle 3P/TTR/<Center point>:' click a point on the screen. The command line displays 'Diameter/<Radius>'. Radius is the default option. If you move the mouse a circle will form determined by the size of the radius you are showing AutoCAD LT. Click on a point. AutoCAD LT draws a circle and the command line is left blank.

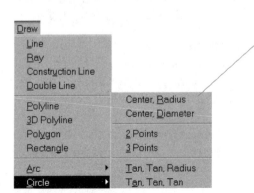

Various options for drawing a circle are shown on this menu

Moving an Entity

 To tell AutoCAD LT you have finished selecting objects, just press the enter key.

To move any entity:

Command line: move, or the alias 'm'

Menu: Modify>Move

Toolbar:

How the command works

AutoCAD LT will need to know what object you want to move. This requires that you select the object or objects. You will then need to specify where you want to pick up the object and lastly where you will place it. If you wish you can give the distance you want to displace or move the object.

 If you miss the object you are trying to select, a box will appear at the cursor. Just move the box so it crosses over the entity and click again.

Using the Move command

Issue the Move command. The command line displays 'Select objects:' and the cursor will change to a pickbox. Place the pickbox over the circle's perimeter and click once. The circle will be highlighted if you succeed. The prompt shows 'Select objects: 1 found', Select objects:'. At this point you press Enter to tell AutoCAD LT that you have finished selecting objects. The command line changes to 'Base point or displacement:'. AutoCAD LT wants to know where you will pick up the object. Click anywhere near or on the circle. The command line displays 'Second point of displacement'. Now you can move the circle by moving the mouse and pick the location you want to position the circle. The command will terminate itself and give you a blank command line.

 If the pickbox is too small, just type 'pickbox' at the command line and increase its value. The default size is 3.

 You can use polar co-ordinates to move an object an exact distance.

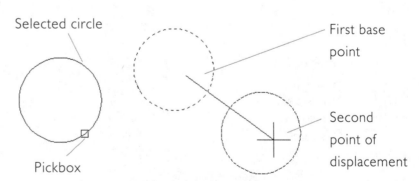

Selected circle

Pickbox

First base point

Second point of displacement

Using Grid and Snap

The F7 key toggles the grid on/off.

The size of the grid may be changed at any time by typing GRID at the command line and entering a new value.

The F9 key toggles the snap on/off.

If you draw outside the grid area you are drawing outside the electronic page you set up.

If the grid setting is too small AutoCAD LT will refuse to display it.

The Grid

The grid is an array of dots placed over the drawing. It is a drawing aid and will not print – it is not part of the drawing. A grid has three main functions: it shows you the size of the electronic sheet you set up; you can snap the cross-hairs to the grid; when you magnify the drawing with the zoom command the distance between the grid points will give you an idea of how much you have magnified the image. The grid can be switched on/off at any time using the status line by double-clicking on it.

Snap

When snap is not active, the cross-hairs move smoothly across the drawing editor. Snap causes the cross-hairs to move in jumps. For example, setting the snap to 25mm will allow you to quickly draw lines of 25mm or multiples thereof. You will not be able to draw between the 25mm setting unless you switch snap off. Often the snap and grid setting are the same (say 25mm) but they do not have to be equal. Snap can be switched on/off from the status line.

Snap is useful for doing a quick sketch with straight edges.

You can also use a special snap to lock on to the elements you have already drawn. See object snap on page 26.

Ortho

Ortho mode allows you to draw lines either vertically or horizontally. The F8 key toggles the ortho mode on and off. You can also double-click on ORTHO on the status line.

The Ortho mode is the equivalent of using a T square in the traditional draughting.

Switches snap grid and ortho modes on/off with a double-click

Drawing Aids

If you do not keep your eye on the command line you will not be able to use AutoCAD LT.

AutoCAD LT has several drawing aids. These are accessed through the menu Tools>Drawing Aids. The dialogue box below is displayed. The Isometric Snap/Grid area within the dialogue box is only used for isometric drawing. It sets up three isoplanes. In this mode a circle will appear elliptical.

It's a good idea to look at this dialogue box before you start working. All the settings can be changed at any time during the drawing procedure. The most important aids are the grid, snap and ortho features.

Switches the Snap on/off

Sets the snap size

Switches the Grid on/off

Sets the size of the grid in the current drawing units

Allows a line to be easily drawn horizontally or vertically

Switches on/off the fills for polyline entities

Represents areas of text with outline

Blips are temporary marks on the screen showing the ends of entities

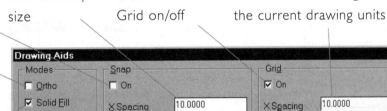

Typing ddrmodes at the command lines will call up the Drawing Aids dialogue box.

When an entity is selected for editing, it is highlighted. This option will switch that highlight on/off

Sets the snap and grid for isometric mode. For standard draughting leave this off

Left, top and right refer to the isoplanes in isometric mode

Snapping to Objects – the Toolbar

HANDY TIP

A toolbar can be dragged to any location on the screen and resized.

By their nature CAD drawings have to be accurate. Joining drawing objects such as lines, arcs and circles should never be done just using your eye. AutoCAD LT has many tools to allow you to lock on to the end of a line or the centre of a circle. These are known as the Object Snap tools and are found on the Object Snap toolbar.

To display the Object Snap Toolbar
View>Toolbars...

The following is displayed:

The tick displays the toolbar

HANDY TIP

The Toolbars dialogue box can be called up by moving the cursor over any existing toolbar and right-clicking.

Click once to place/remove the tick

List of available toolbars

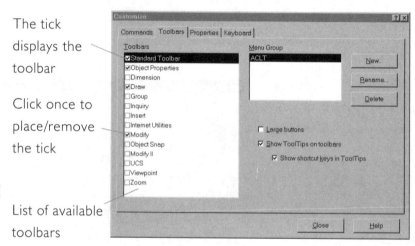

The Object Snap Toolbar

BEWARE

Do not use snap and object snap at the same time.

tracking   intersection   perpendicular   none

endpoint   quadrant   node

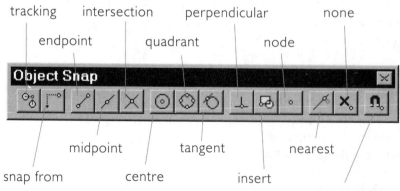

snap from   midpoint   centre   tangent   insert   nearest   object snap settings

Snapping to Objects – an Example

If you fail to read what is displayed at the command line, you will not be able to draw with accuracy.

Always use the object snap to ensure accuracy.

Try typing some of the commands instead of clicking on them from menus: it will make you more command-line aware.

Never try to join objects by relying on your eye. Always snap to objects.

Display the Object Snap toolbar (see page 26). Draw a line and a circle near each other on the screen. Now move the circle using object snap to the end of the line so that the centre of the circle is located exactly on the end of the line, as follows:

1 Issue the Move command and read the command line.

2 Pick the circle in response to 'select objects'.

3 Press Enter to tell AutoCAD LT that there is nothing else you want to select.

4 In response to 'Base point or displacement' click on 'Snap to Center' from the Object Snap toolbar. The command line now displays 'cen of' (meaning centre of).

5 Move the mouse down to the periphery of the selected circle. When a small red selection circle appears at the centre of the selected circle, click the left mouse button.

6 AutoCAD LT will pick up the circle at its centre point and the command line will display 'Second point of displacement:'

7 Click on 'Snap to Endpoint' from the Object Snap toolbar and move the cursor down over the line towards the end you want to place the circle. The command line will display 'endp of'.

8 A red selection box will appear towards one end of the line. Click when you see this. The circle will lock into position.

Running Object Snap Tools

BEWARE

If you find the cursor behaving in a way you do not understand, try switching off the object snap. It's easy to forget you have it on.

In situations where you are doing a lot of editing, you may find that you are constantly selecting from the Object Snap toolbar. You can overcome this by setting up a running object snap. This allows you to preset and switch on the object snaps you frequently use. When the running object snap is switched on, the cursor will automatically select those snaps as soon as you approach an entity.

Setting up the object snap

Command line: osnap, or the alias 'os'

Menu: Tools>Object Snap Settings

Status Bar: Double-click on OSNAP at the bottom of the screen

                    Or press the F3 key

Click here

Click here

Object snap
dialogue box

HANDY TIP

Once the running object snap is set up, it can be toggled on/off by double-clicking OSNAP on the status line.

Place an X in the
object snaps you
want to use

Resize the aperture by
pulling on the slider
button

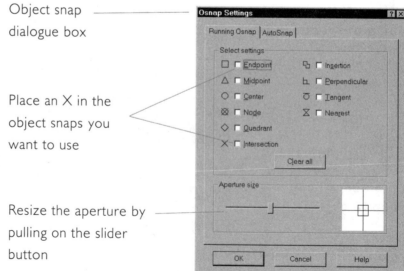

Accuracy and Speed

In this chapter, you'll learn how to speed up drawing and editing by using some of AutoCAD LT's sophisticated tools. Aliases, aerial views and snapping to objects will increase speed and accuracy dramatically. It is worth concentrating on these until they are mastered. Using co-ordinate input is essential for any work that requires specific dimensions. You may think you can survive without grips – until you know how to use them! They save time and ensure accuracy.

Covers

Chapter Three

Opening an Existing Drawing

Command line: open, or 'op'

Menu: File>Open

 Double-clicking on a file name will automatically open it into AutoCAD LT.

Toolbar:

Once the command is issued, AutoCAD LT may want to know if it should save changes to the drawing on the screen.

Means save the current drawing now

Means do not save the additions made to the work

Cancel the command and return me to this drawing

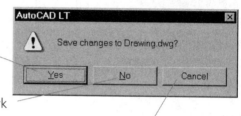

If a dialogue box does not appear, AutoCAD LT has already saved the current work. The Select File dialogue box will then open.

This is the current folder you are looking in

Click to open the selected drawing

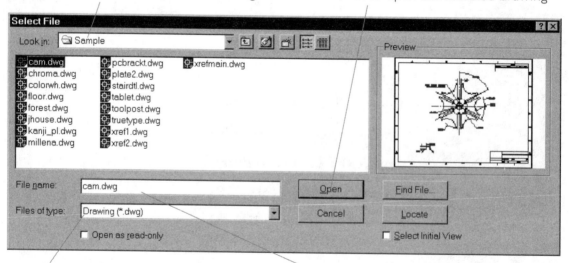

Shows the type of file listed – you may also view dxf and template files

Type the file name you want to open in here or click on it in the list

Using Co-ordinate Input

AutoCAD LT has several ways to input co-ordinates to specify the length of objects, or their angle of orientation. Co-ordinate input can also be used to specify the distance over which objects can be copied, moved or stretched. Gaps can be made in objects – eg, by inputting the width of the gap in polar co-ordinates. Absolute, relative and polar co-ordinates will be described below.

Absolute co-ordinates

This co-ordinate system relies on the location of the origin 0,0. The origin is normally located at the bottom left of the screen. The X and Y axis meet at the origin. An absolute co-ordinate is input as two numbers separated by a comma. The first number is the distance along the X axis and the second number the distance on the Y axis.

For example, to draw a line from the origin:

Command: L	(Type L and press Enter)
LINE From point: 0,0	(Type in the 0,0 and Enter)
To point: 100,100	(Type in the 100,100 and Enter)
To point:	(Press Enter to end the line command)

Relative co-ordinates

This co-ordinate system relies on the location of the last point entered. The @ symbol is entered before the co-ordinate. It means from the last position. A co-ordinate @45,67 specifies a location 45 units along the X axis and 67 units along the Y axis *relative* to the last location.

Polar co-ordinates

This co-ordinate system allows you to specify a distance and angle from the last point. It takes the format:

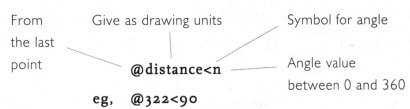

From the last point   Give as drawing units   Symbol for angle

@distance<n   Angle value between 0 and 360

eg,   **@322<90**

Co-ordinate Input – Examples

Polar co-ordinates can be used any time that AutoCAD LT asks for a displacement or a new point. To follow these examples, set a page size of 420 by 297 in decimal units.

HANDY TIP

You do not have to pick the first point of displacement on the object you are moving.

Drawing a line – absolute and polar co-ordinates

Issue the Line command. Read the command line and enter an absolute co-ordinate of 0,0 and press Enter. A line will run from the origin out to the cross hairs. In response to 'To point:' type in the polar co-ordinate @50<45. A line 50 mm long at an angle of 45 degrees will be drawn. Continue with the following values in response to 'To point:': @100<0, @200<90, @100<180, @100<270. Press Enter to finish the command.

BEWARE

If you accidentally terminate the current command, then use object snap to pick up from the end of the last line endpoint and just proceed with the polar co-ordinates.

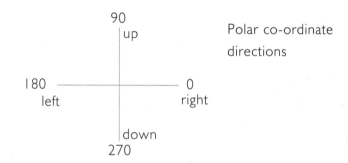

Polar co-ordinate directions

Moving a line by polar co-ordinates

Let us imagine you have to move the right vertical line 25mm to the right (0 degrees direction). Issue the Move command. Click on the right vertical line when asked to 'Select objects'. Press Enter to tell AutoCAD LT that you have finished selecting objects. In response to 'Base point or displacement' click anywhere on the screen (click near the line). In response to 'Second point of displacement' type in @25<0 and press Enter. The line will be moved 25mm to the right.

REMEMBER

Direction is input at an angle in polar co-ordinates.

Try doing this with the Copy command.

Using Zoom and Pan

Pan is one of the few commands where you do not need to look at the command line.

Zoom allows you to change the magnification of your view of the drawing. Pan allows you to move around the drawing without changing the magnification. Zoom and pan are aids to help you work with the drawing.

Pan icon: just click on it, move out onto the drawing editor, hold down the left mouse button and drag. If you have a mouse with a wheel between the buttons try rotating this

You can pan and zoom by clicking on the right mouse button and selecting from the menu.

Zoom icon: just click on it, move onto the drawing, hold down the left mouse button. As you drag the cursor up the screen you magnify the drawing (+ sign); as you drag the cursor down the screen you zoom away from the drawing (- sign)

Zoom window icon: this allows you to select a window or box around the area you want to magnify. Respond by selecting a point on the screen and pull a window around the objects you want to magnify

If you get lost press the Esc key and try again.

Zoom previous icon: AutoCAD LT remembers the previous level of magnification and will return you to it when you click on the icon

You can pan and zoom using the command line. Type zoom or z and pan or p and press Enter.

Exits from the zoom options and blanks the command line

This will zoom to fit the complete drawing on the screen

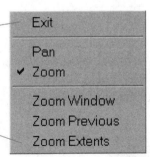

Aerial View

Aerial view is exceptionally useful if you are working on a drawing that occupies a large area. It enables you to view the whole drawing in a small window within the drawing editor. Panning and zooming in the smaller aerial view window will be reflected in the drawing editor. The aerial view window can be dragged around the screen, minimized, maximized and closed in the usual manner for all windows.

The aerial view can be called up by typing 'dsviewer' at the command line.

Aerial view is most useful for large complex drawings.

Aerial view icon

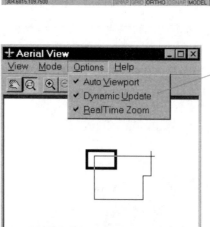

Aerial view window

Overall view of the drawing

Area of the drawing shown in the drawing editor

You cannot draw or edit inside the aerial view window.

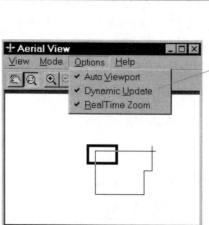

The aerial view can immediately show changes made to the drawing in the drawing editor if the Dynamic Update is ticked under the Options menu on the aerial view window

The Purge Command

To purge a drawing is to remove any references in the drawing to unused linetypes, text styles layers, blocks, etc. A drawing which has been purged is often smaller in size and much more stable than an unpurged drawing. It is good practice to purge a drawing before you store it permanently or give it to another person. Always purge a drawing before you send it via e-mail, for example.

A drawing which has never been purged can become unstable.

While constructing a drawing you may make a layer or load a linetype and find that you never use it. Purge will remove any reference to them.

To issue the command

Type 'purge' at the command line and press enter. The option 'All' will prompt you for blocks, layers, etc. The other options allow you to select individual objects.

The drop-down option is under the File menu 'Drawing Utilities'.

A plus sign shows that items under the selected heading can be purged. Click on the plus symbol to see the items.

Purge will not remove AutoCAD LT default settings such as the continuous linetype.

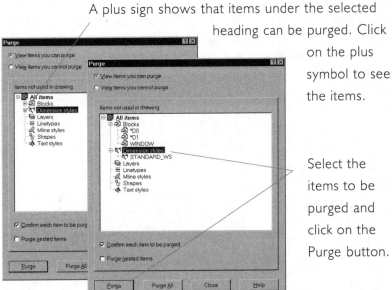

Select the items to be purged and click on the Purge button.

Purge will not delete anything which is used in the drawing.

Purge needs to be run several times as it only works to one level of reference at a time. Keep purging until you see the message 'No unreferenced x to purge'.

How to Select Objects

Objects in the drawing editor need to be selected regularly while drawing and editing. Using the pickbox to select individual elements is a commonly used technique. However there are several other ways which are particularly useful for selecting several objects. Some of these methods are described here.

Imagine that the command line displays 'Select objects:' The following selection methods work:

Don't limit yourself to the same selection options all the time. Being familiar with several will add speed and accuracy to your work.

1   All: this selects all objects in the drawing except those on layers that are thawed (see Chapter Seven, *Working with Layers*). The complete drawing will highlight. This is useful if you wish to move the whole drawing to a new location on the page.

2   l: l is for last. The last object you worked on will be selected.

3   p: p is for previous. The last objects you selected will be selected.

4   f: f is for fence. You can select points on the screen through which AutoCAD LT draws a fence line. Objects which the fence cross are selected.

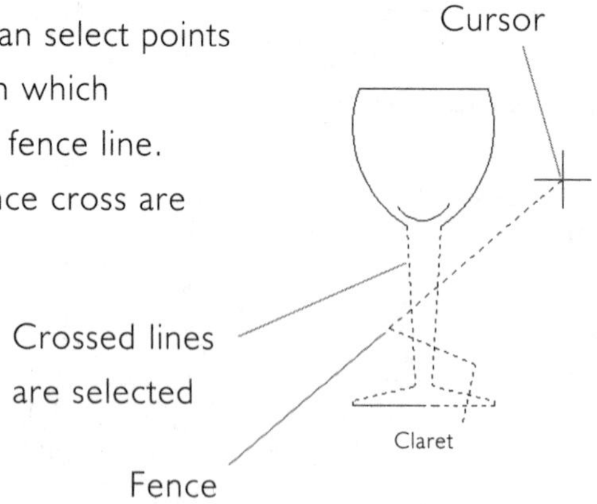

Cursor

Crossed lines are selected

Claret

Fence

5   cp: cp means crossing polygon. This time the 'fence' is called a polygon. Construct it the same way as the fence. Objects selected either cross the polygon or are completely inside it.

...cont'd

HANDY TIP

Don't bother pressing 'c' for a crossing window, just click and move the cursor from right to left for a crossing box.

6 c: c is for crossing. This selection method involves pulling a window around the objects. Those objects crossing the window or completely within it are selected. If you respond to the 'Select objects' prompt by just clicking a point on the drawing and moving to the left and up, a crossing selection window is formed automatically.

7 w: w is for window. Pull a window around the object(s). Those objects completely within the window will be highlighted. If you don't respond to the 'select objects' prompt with 'w', just drag a window from right to left. This will automatically form a selection window.

HANDY TIP

The crossing window is displayed with a dashed line; the window method shows a window displayed by a continuous line.

8 wp: this is a polygon window. Objects must be completely within the polygon for selection.

9 r: r is for remove. This invaluable option allows you to deselect objects which you accidentally selected.

The crossing window is a dashed box

All the objects crossing the windows will be selected along with those completely inside the window

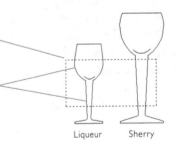

Liqueur   Sherry

HANDY TIP

You can mix the selection methods. For example, start with a crossing window and continue with a fence or a single click selection.

The complete selection window is a continuous box

Only this arc will be selected

Grips – the Little Blue Boxes

You have probably experienced these little blue boxes appearing on objects in the drawing editor. They are called Grips. Pressing the Esc key will remove them. The grips appear if you select an object while the command line is blank. They appear at specific points on an object such as the endpoints and midpoint of a line. Grips can be dragged to perform actions such as rotating, moving or scaling the object.

 Grips can be applied to several entities at once by dragging a window around them.

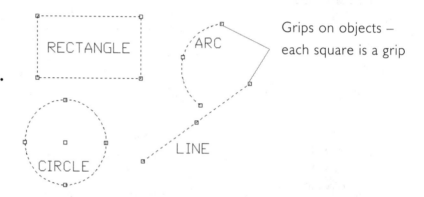

Grips on objects – each square is a grip

 Right-clicking when a grip is highlighted will bring up the commands associated with it.

To call up the grips dialogue box use Tools>Grips... or at the command line type ddgrips. The grips can also be switched on/off by entering 1 for 'on' and 0 for 'off' in response to the typed command grips.

A tick here allows the grips to function

Sets the colour for selected and unselected grips

Sets the size of the grip box

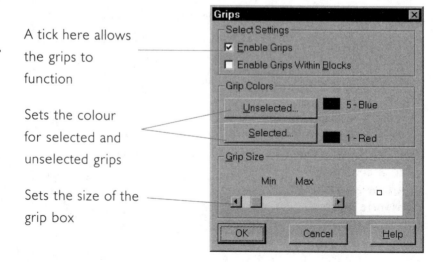

How to Use the Grips

Grips allow you to apply the following commands to an object: Stretch, Move, Rotate, Scale and Mirror.

To try out these options, draw a separate line and circle.

Default options are always shown inside angle brackets <>.

Moving a circle with grips

Without issuing a command, click on the circle. Grips will appear. Now click on the centre-point grip. It will become a solid colour (red is the default). The command line shows:

STRETCH

<Stretch to point>/Base point/Copy/Undo/eXit:

To see the other commands press the spacebar or the Enter key. Keep pressing it until you see the Move command. The command line will then show:

<Move to point>/Base point/Copy/Undo/eXit:

Cycle through the Grip options by pressing either the spacebar or the Enter key.

The default option is shown in angled brackets. When you move the cursor the circle will move with it. At this point you can do one of three things:

- just click a point on the screen to reposition the circle
- use polar co-ordinates to re-locate it accurately
- use Object Snap to snap to another object

To remove the grips press the Esc key twice.

Stretching a line with grips

Select the line. The grips will appear. Click on one of the endpoints to highlight a grip. Press the spacebar or the Enter key until you find:

STRETCH

Use polar co-ordinates or Object Snap in conjunction with grips for greater accuracy.

<Stretch to point>/Base point/Copy/Undo/eXit:

At this point you can do one of three things:

- just click a point on the screen to stretch the line
- use polar co-ordinates to stretch it a specific distance
- use Object Snap to snap to another object

System Variables

System variables hold specific settings or values that affect how the AutoCAD LT system works. By changing a variable you specify how a command might function or how the AutoCAD LT screen looks. Here are some useful variables.

Blipmode

This controls the display of small '+' symbols called blips, at selection points on the screen. It is set to 'off' in AutoCAD LT 97 and 98. Try switching it on and draw a line to see the effect. At the command line type 'Blipmode' and press the spacebar or Enter. Type 'On' or 'Off'. The default setting is shown in angled brackets.

Blips are not part of the drawing. They will not be printed. The Redraw command (or just R and Enter) removes blips.

Mirrtext

This variable controls how text is mirrored when you use the Mirror command. If text is mirrored when the variable is set to 1 (the default value), the text will appear inverted (exactly as it would appear in a real mirror). If the Mirrtext variable is set to 0, the text will appear normal (legible). Type 'Mirrtext' at the command line to change it.

Ucsicon

The image of the X and Y axis at the bottom left of the screen is controlled by this system variable. It can be switched on or off by typing 'Ucsicon' at the command line.

Filedia

Controls the display of the dialogue boxes associated with file commands such as the Save and Save As. There are two settings – 1 causes the boxes to be displayed (this is the default); 0 prevents their display. If a dialogue box is not displayed you must read the command line to save the files. Type 'Filedia' to change the settings.

Offsetdist

Allows you to set a default value for the offset command. Type 'Offsetdist' and enter a new value in drawing units.

Advanced Drawing Commands

In this chapter, you'll learn how to use some of AutoCAD LT's more advanced commands to create complex objects. Construction lines such as rays and xlines will help you to place objects on the drawing more accurately. They are designed to be quick to draw. The commands for creating polyline curves, circles and straight line segments are looked at in detail. Lastly you will draw a door arc as it might be constructed in an architectural drawing.

Chapter Four

Covers

Ray

Rays can be constructed using different linetypes such as dotted or dash-dot (see *Linetypes*, page 92).

How the command works

A ray is a line which has a starting point and extends off to infinity in a single direction. They are used to help construct a drawing rather than be objects as a part of the drawing. When the command is issued, AutoCAD LT will ask for the ray's starting point and then for another point through which the ray will run.

Command line: ray

Menu: Draw>Ray

Toolbar:

The command in action

When the command is issued the response is:

Right-clicking with the mouse over the drawing editor will allow you to repeat the last command.

From point: Select a point. You can use object snap or type an absolute co-ordinate

Through point: Select a point. You can use object snap or type a polar co-ordinate

Finish the command by pressing Enter or the space bar.

Rays emanating from a point. Rays have an endpoint for object snap but no midpoint.

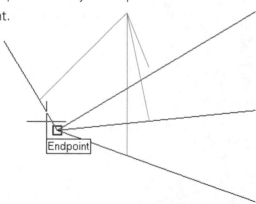

Endpoint

The properties associated with a ray can be modified using the command Ddmodify.

Construction Line or Xline

You can snap to the root of the xline using the Object Snap midpoint.

How the command works

A construction or xline is a line that runs to infinity in two directions. As in the construction of any type of line you need two points to define it. The first point you pick becomes the 'root' of the construction line. There are many ways to pick the points for constructing the xline, including the Object Snap modes.

Command line: xline, or the alias 'xl'

Menu: Draw>Construction Line

Toolbar:

The command in action

When the command is issued you have to select the first point or root. The default is to just pick a point on the screen or use object snap. Five other options are offered. To select one of these options type the capitalized letter from the list. The options are shown below:

Constructs a horizontal or vertical xline. Use object snap to draw it through a specific point.

Draws the xline parallel to an existing line – decide the distance

XLINE Hor/Ver/Ang/Bisect/Offset/<From point>:

Use these construction lines sparingly, otherwise your drawing can quickly become cluttered with lines.

Specify an angle for the xline

Bisect an existing angle

Default option – just pick a point or use object snap

Through point: Select a point. You can use object snap or type a polar co-ordinate. Finish the command by pressing Enter or the space bar.

Double Line – Overview

How the command works

A double line consists of two parallel lines. They can be used to represent cavity walls in a building, for example. You can tell AutoCAD LT how far the two lines are from each other. In drawing the double line you select beginning and end points in the usual ways. Double lines can have caps at either end or none at all. All the lines that compose a double line can be edited and erased independently.

HANDY TIP

You can enter the width of a double line either before or after you select the start point.

Command line: dline, or the alias 'dl'

Menu: Draw>Double Line

Toolbar:

Each of these double lines was drawn from left to right

Width is 15 units

End cap

Caps set to None

Start cap

Endcaps set to Both

HANDY TIP

The most useful options are Width, Caps and Break.

The command in action

When the command is issued the response is:

Break/Caps/Dragline/Offset/Snap/Undo/Width/<start point>:

The default option is to pick a point (use object snap if you like). To enter a width type W and press Enter. The value you input is in drawing units. Once the first point is selected the command line options change to:

HANDY TIP

Note how two of the options begin with 'C' so you have to type the first two letters to distinguish them.

Arc/Break/CAps/CLose/Dragline/Snap/Undo/Width/<next point>:

Continue selecting points. Press Enter to finish the command.

Double Line Options in Detail

Break/Caps/Dragline/Offset/Snap/Undo/Width/:

The Offset option allows you to start the double line a specific distance from some object or base point.

Break

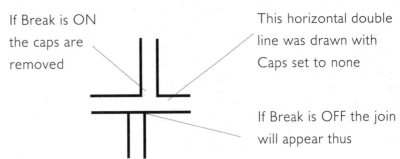

If Break is ON the caps are removed

This horizontal double line was drawn with Caps set to none

If Break is OFF the join will appear thus

Caps

The Snap option will allow you to snap to an existing object.

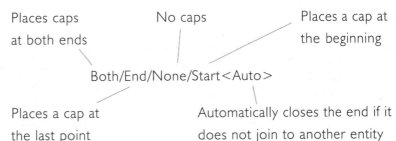

Places caps at both ends

No caps

Places a cap at the beginning

Both/End/None/Start<Auto>

Places a cap at the last point

Automatically closes the end if it does not join to another entity

Dragline

Because double lines have a distance between them, you need to be able to tell AutoCAD LT how the two lines are constructed when you snap to the end or mid of other entities. The Dragline option allows this.

The Undo option allows segments of what you have drawn to be removed while remaining in the command.

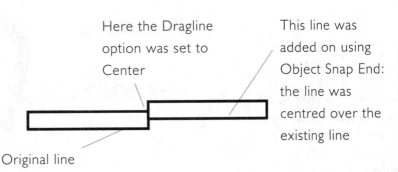

Here the Dragline option was set to Center

This line was added on using Object Snap End: the line was centred over the existing line

Original line

Polylines

 HANDY TIP

The Close option draws the polyline back to the first point picked. It has special editing properties.

How the command works

Polylines are quite special. Unlike the standard line they can have a width and they can follow a curved path. Polylines need special editing options to modify them. To draw the polyline you need to give it a start and end point. Other options such as the width must be selected after the first point is chosen. You can give different widths for the beginning and end points of a polyline. AutoCAD LT will taper the line from one width to the other. Polylines can be turned into curves.

Command line: pline, or the alias 'pl'

Menu: Draw>Polyline

Toolbar:

 HANDY TIP

Use a polyline to create arrow heads.

The command in action

When the command is issued the response is:

From point: Pick in the usual way

Arc/Close/Halfwidth/Length/Undo/Width/<Endpoint of line>:

Select the Width option. Enter a beginning width. Press Enter and type in an ending width. Try drawing a few lines.

Beginning width of 10 units

Ending width of 10 units

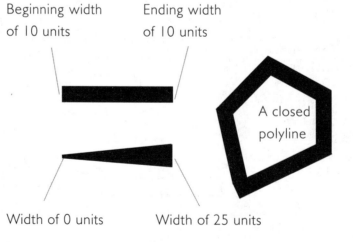

A closed polyline

Width of 0 units

Width of 25 units

 HANDY TIP

You can specify a halfwidth – this is the width from the central axis of the polyline to the edge.

Polyline Shapes

Try turning the Fill option off by typing Fill at the command line and responding with 'off'.

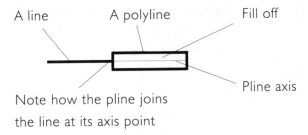

A line   A polyline   Fill off

Pline axis

Note how the pline joins the line at its axis point

Polylines can contain arcs. When you use the Arc option, select the arc endpoints and return to straight plines using the option 'l'.

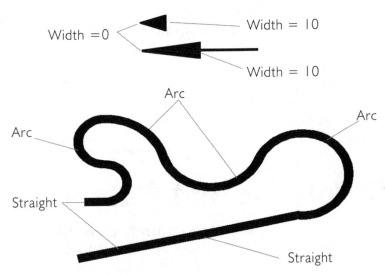

Width =0   Width = 10

Width = 10

Arc

Arc

Arc

Straight

Straight

The Length option allows a polyline to be increased by entering a value in units.

The prompt is 'Length of line:'

Just type a value and the line will be extended at the same angle as the existing polyline.

Fill can be on or off for all the polylines in the drawing. You cannot have some polylines with fill on and others with it off.

This shape was drawn with one execution of the command. The width was changed after each segment was drawn. The starting and ending width of each segment is the same.

Rectangles

How the command works

A rectangle is composed of four polylines. You simply pick two points to draw it. The sides of the rectangle are always parallel to the horizontal and vertical sides of the screen.

Command line: rectang

Menu: Draw>Rectangle

Toolbar:

The command in action

Issue the command. Pick two points:

 You can object snap to the sides of the rectangle.

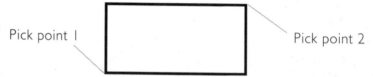

Pick point 1   Pick point 2

3D Polyline and Rectangle

How the command works

3D polylines are similar to the standard pline. The differences are (1) they are drawn in 3D space and so can take a Z coordinate, and (2) they can only be converted to special types of curves.

Command line: pline, or the alias 'pl'

Menu: Draw>Polyline

Toolbar: None

The command in action

When the command is issued the response is:

From point: Pick as usual

Close/Undo/<Endpoint of line>:

The options are similar to those for the normal polyline.

Polygons

Polygons are made from polylines. You can edit them using the pedit command.

How the command works

A polygon is an enclosed shape with 3 to 1024 sides. You can draw a polygon in two basic ways. Define one side of the polygon and AutoCAD LT will draw the others, or pick the centre of the polygon and AutoCAD LT will draw the sides inside or outside a circle.

Command line: polygon, or the alias 'pg'

Menu: Draw>Polygon

Toolbar:

The command in action

Issue the command. AutoCAD LT will want to know the number of sides in the polygon. Type in a value and press enter. The response is:

Edge/<Centre of polygon>: (Press Enter to accept the default)

Inscribed in circle/Circumscribed about circle(I/C)<I>:

You can object snap a line onto the mid point or end point of the sides of the polyline.

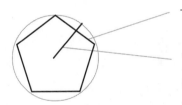

This is an inscribed 5 sided polygon

The radius can be input as a value or picked with the cursor

Even though a polygon can be defined around or inside a circle, you cannot object snap to the centre of a polygon.

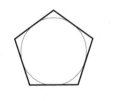

This is a circumscribed 5 sided polygon

This is a 5 sided polygon from a straight edge

Arcs

How the command works

There are many ways to draw an arc, each of which is listed on the drop-down menu below. Arcs are parts of circles, and all arcs have a beginning and an end point. AutoCAD LT uses these points in three techniques. All arcs have a centre: this is used in four techniques. Three techniques use the idea of an angle to specify the distance the arc spans.

REMEMBER

Arcs are made from a circle. Three points are needed for AutoCAD LT to draw the arc.

Command line: arc

Menu: Draw>Arc

Toolbar:

New in

LT 98

Arc Options

3 Points
Start, Center, End
Start, Center, Angle
Start, Center, Length
Start, End, Angle
Start, End, Direction
Start, End, Radius
Center, Start, End
Center, Start, Angle
Center, Start, Length
Continue

The command in action

Here are two of the techniques:

HANDY TIP

Arcs can be a bit difficult to master. Concentrate on one (perhaps the Start Center, End) until you can predict the results.

1   The Start, Center, End option.

Start, Center, End

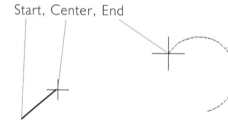

The arc is drawn in an anticlockwise direction

2   The Start, Center, Angle option

Start, Center, Angle

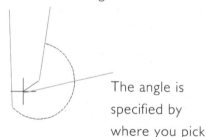

The angle is specified by where you pick

Negative angles give a clockwise arc

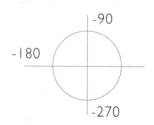

How to Draw a Door Arc

This is the type of arc that is used by an architect to describe the sweep of a door.

An angle that is negative sweeps an arc clockwise.

To follow this set up a drawing using decimal units with a sheet size of about 2000mm by 2000mm. Use double lines to draw a wall and a single line to represent the door at 90 degrees to the wall. The door gap must also be 900mm. The arc will be drawn using the option Start, Center, Angle.

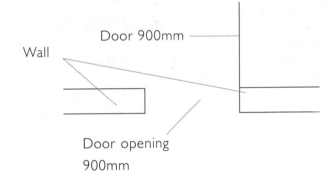

Door 900mm

Wall

Door opening 900mm

Use the object snap modes to position the arc Start and Center points.

Command sequence
Click Start, Center, Angle.

Pick the start point using Object Snap End to locate the top of the door.

For the centre pick where the door meets the wall using Object Snap Midpoint.

The angle option is used to describe the distance the arc sweeps.

When asked for the angle, type in 90. This sweeps an arc anti clockwise through a distance of 90 degrees.

Angle is 90 (anticlockwise)

Start of the arc

Centre of the circle that makes the arc Midpoint

Donuts

If you erase a donut (or other object) it may appear that other parts of the drawing have also been erased. By typing 'r' for Redraw the screen is refreshed and you should see the unerased objects.

How the command works

Donuts are circles made from polylines. Donuts have two diameters. The area between the diameters is filled solid if the Fill command is set to On.

Command line: donut, or the alias 'do'

Menu: Draw>Donut

Toolbar:

The command in action

You are simply asked for the inside and outside diameters. The default options are shown in angled brackets. The centre point can be picked using Object Snap or by just clicking on it. The Donut command will continue until Enter or the spacebar is pressed to finish it.

You must type 'Regen' after you change the Fill command. This allows you to see the effect on the donuts (or polylines).

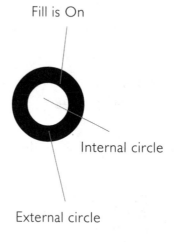

Fill is On

Internal circle

External circle

A donut with an inside diameter of 0 becomes a solid circle

Internal diameter is 0

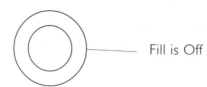

Fill is Off

Splines

HANDY TIP **When experiment-ing with spline curves, use other drawing objects to snap on to. This will help you to remember the points you picked and consequently understand how the curves are formed.**

How the command works

A spline is a curve. To create one, you pick several points on the screen. AutoCAD LT will draw the curve through the first and last points, and as close as it can to the points in between.

Command line: spline

Menu: Draw>Spline

Toolbar:

The command in action

You are asked for each point. Pick the points in the usual way and press enter three times to end the command. The splines below were drawn with different tolerances. To try it, draw two lines – one vertical and one horizontal.

HANDY TIP **If the splines are not going the way you expect, check the tolerance setting.**

Different Techniques:

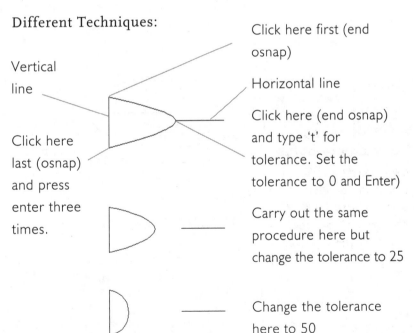

Vertical line

Click here last (osnap) and press enter three times.

Click here first (end osnap)

Horizontal line

Click here (end osnap) and type 't' for tolerance. Set the tolerance to 0 and Enter)

Carry out the same procedure here but change the tolerance to 25

Change the tolerance here to 50

BEWARE **AutoCAD LT will remember and use the last tolerance you set.**

Notice how the spline always goes through the first and last point picked. It 'attempts' to go through the second point when the tolerance is above o.

Ellipses

How the command works

An ellipse has a long (or major) axis and a short (or minor) axis. AutoCAD LT draws an ellipse by asking you to select or specify the length of the axis. Whichever is the longest is the major axis. In other words, you don't have to say which is major or minor: AutoCAD LT just lets you draw.

AutoCAD LT will take the longest axis as the major and the shorter one as the minor axis.

Command line: ellipse, or the alias 'el'

Menu: Draw>Ellipse

Toolbar:

The command in action

The command line default prompt is ':<Axis endpoint ɪ>:' Once the point is picked you have set the centre of the ellipse. The prompt now asks for the 'Axis endpoint 2'. This will determine the length of the first axis. The prompt for '<Other axis distance>' describes the ellipse fully.

The length of the axis can be input as polar co-ordinates.

At this stage the prompt is 'Other axis distance'

This becomes the minor axis in this case

The 'Center' option allows you to pick the centre of the ellipse first. You then need to tell AutoCAD LT the length of the axes.

If you draw in Isometric mode you can create isocircles. These are really ellipses pretending to be circles viewed at an angle.

How to Edit Objects

In this chapter, many of AutoCAD LT's powerful editing commands are introduced. We will also look at the array command, which has a new interface in release LT 98.

Covers

Chapter Five

Erase and the Revision Cloud

See pages 36 and 37 on how to select objects.

How the command works

Erase will remove objects from the drawing. To use it efficiently you must master the art of object selection. Objects selected to be erased will highlight. If you want to erase part of an object you will have to use a command like Break to break it into two entities. Enter must be pressed to terminate the command.

Command line: erase, or the alias 'e'

Menu: Modify>Erase

If you select one object too many with the Erase command, you can type U to undo the selection and still stay in the command.

Toolbar:

The command in action

Issue the Erase command. Select the objects and press enter to finish the command. Remember you can mix the selection methods.

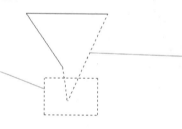

Crossing selection box is used here

Highlighted objects will be erased when you press Enter

Revision Cloud with a small arc

Revision Cloud – AutoCAD LT 98 only

When looking at a plotted drawing you may 'mark' a section to be revised with a pen or pencil. You can simulate this procedure in AutoCAD LT 98 by using the Revision Cloud. A Revision Cloud is drawn using arcs.

Command line: revcloud

Toolbar:

You can specify the arc size (use A and Enter to select the option) and simply draw the cloud by moving the pointing device. AutoCAD LT 98 will close the cloud once you near the beginning.

Revision Cloud with a large arc

Copy Objects around the Drawing

How the command works

Copy works in a very similar way to move. AutoCAD LT will ask you to select the object(s) you want to copy and then the base point for picking the objects up and finally the place where you want to position the objects. If you want to make several copies of the object then use the Multiple option. In this Multiple mode, AutoCAD LT will allow you to place as many copies in the drawing as you like.

Command line: copy, or the alias 'cp'

Menu: Modify>Copy

Toolbar:

If you want to copy an object to a very specific location in the drawing, use object snap to pick up the object and object snap to position it.

The command in action

Issue the Copy command. Select the objects and press Enter to finish the selection. Remember, you can mix the selection methods. Pick a base point on or near the objects to copy and select the second point in a similar way.

If you're using the same text in several positions on the drawing, use Copy with the Multiple option to make any number of copies of the text.

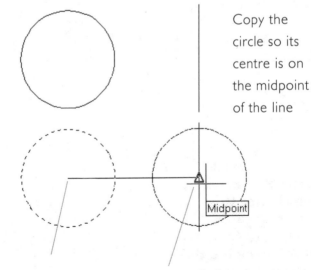

Copy the circle so its centre is on the midpoint of the line

Select the circle

Base point is the center of the circle – use Object Snap

Second base point is the midpoint of the line – use Object Snap Midpoint

Mirror

HANDY TIP

If you mirror objects with Ortho on, you can only mirror at 90 or 180 degrees. This can be very useful. Try it, and when asked for the second mirror axis point, click with the mouse to lock the image.

HANDY TIP

Mirror is a Grips option. Highlight a grip and press the spacebar until you see Mirror (see page 39).

HANDY TIP

If you don't want the text inverted when you mirror, then change the system variable Mirrtext to 0 before you issue the command. See page 40 on *System Variables*.

How the command works

The command is used to mirror object(s) across an axis. You select the object you want to mirror, tell AutoCAD LT where the mirror axis is and AutoCAD LT will do the rest. The command has two interesting features. Firstly you don't actually have to have an axis drawn on the screen: you can use any two points which define an axis. Secondly you can tell AutoCAD LT to delete the object(s) you're going to mirror so that you end up with one inverted copy.

Command line: mirror, or the alias 'mi'

Menu: Modify>Mirror

Toolbar:

The command in action

Issue the Mirror command. Select the objects and press Enter to finish the selection. Remember, you can mix the selection methods. The mirror axis is defined by any two points on the line. Pick the points when AutoCAD LT asks 'First point on mirror line' and 'Second point'. If you accept the default to 'Delete old objects?<N>' the objects will be mirrored.

Use Object Snap to pick points on the mirror axis

In this case the mirror axis was defined between the midpoints of the top and bottom horizontal lines

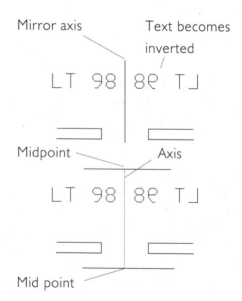

Offset

BEWARE

Polylines are offset from the axis that runs down through the centre of the pline.

How the command works

Offset will make a copy of objects parallel to existing objects. It is one of the most useful commands in AutoCAD LT and is well worth mastering. You will be asked what you want to offset and then the distance to offset and finally the side of the original object you want the offset to occur on.

Command line: offset, or the alias 'of'

Menu: Modify>Offset

Toolbar:

The command in action

REMEMBER

AutoCAD LT keeps the last offset distance as the default.

Issue the Offset command. AutoCAD LT immediately asks for the distance you want to offset – 'Offset distance or Through <default>:' Enter a distance and select the object. You can only select one object to offset at a time. Finally select the side to offset the object.

The inner circle was produced by offsetting the outer one by 10 units

The left line was offset by 10 units on the right

BEWARE

If you offset a polyline make sure that the offset distance is more than the halfwidth distance of the polyline, otherwise you won't see it.

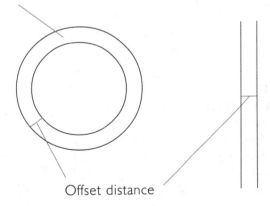

Offset distance

Rotate

How the command works

You can rotate any objects around a central rotation point. Select the objects to rotate, then specify the base point about which the rotation is to occur (which can be on the object itself) and lastly the angle through which the rotation should occur. A positive rotation angle means anticlockwise. A negative angle is clockwise.

HANDY TIP **Rotate is a Grips option. Highlight a grip and press the spacebar until you see Rotate (see page 39).**

Command line: rotate, or the alias 'ro'

Menu: Modify>Rotate

Toolbar:

The command in action

Issue the Rotate command. Select the objects and press Enter to finish the selection. You can mix the selection methods. Now AutoCAD LT will ask for the 'Base point:'. Pick a point. Type a value in response to the prompt for 'Rotation angle'.

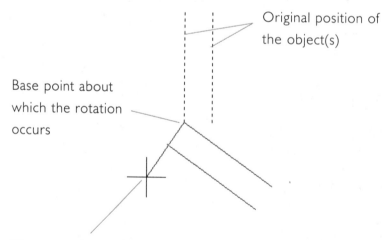

Original position of the object(s)

Base point about which the rotation occurs

HANDY TIP **The reference angle allows a rotation from some existing angle – usually of the object being rotated.**

The cursor is attached to this base point. As it is moved the objects rotate. Type an angle if you like or just click on a point on the screen

Scale

Scale is a Grips option. Highlight a grip and press the spacebar until you see Scale (see page 39).

How the command works

Objects can be scaled up or down from a base point. A scale value of 1 leaves the object as it is. A value of 0.5 halves its size while a value of 2 doubles it.

Command line: scale, or the alias 'sc'

Menu: Modify>Scale

Toolbar:

The command in action

Issue the Scale command. Select the objects and press enter to finish the selection. You can mix the selection methods. The base option can be on or near the object. Object Snap may be used.

If you scale an object that has been dimensioned, the value of the dimension will change only if associative dimensioning is switched on.

Text whilst being scaled is highlighted

Base point   Original text

A scaled object increases or decreases its size from the select base point.

The Scale command should not be used to produce a drawing on the correct size before it is printed. The Print command has a separate Plotting Scale option.

Stretch

HANDY TIP

Polar co-ordinates are very useful in stretching. In the example here, you could stretch the lines by 10 units by entering @10<0 when asked for the 'Second point of displacement'.

How the command works

The Stretch command either lengthens or shortens objects. A crossing window must cross the objects you want to stretch. Any object which lies completely within the selection window is moved. AutoCAD LT will ask you for a base point, which it uses to calculate the amount of stretch.

Command line: Stretch

Menu: Modify>Stretch

Toolbar:

The command in action

Issue the Stretch command. Select the objects by pulling a crossing window so that it cuts or crosses the object you want to stretch.

BEWARE

Objects completely inside the selection box will not be stretched – only moved.

Select objects:	Pull a crossing window or crossing polygon from right to left
Base point of displacement:	Pick a point on/near the object
Second point of displacement:	Click on a point with the cursor or use co-ordinates or object snap to another object

BEWARE

If you do not use a crossing window or polygon you will not be able to stretch the objects.

1 Lines to be stretched

3 Stretched objects – note the changed dimension

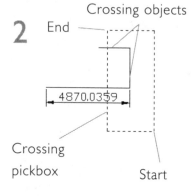

2 Crossing objects

Crossing pickbox

Start

Lengthen

If an object is closed – like a double line or a polyline – it cannot be lengthened.

How the command works

This command will allow you to increase or decrease the length of objects. Basically you just select the objects and then tell AutoCAD LT how you want to increase/decrease the length of the objects. There are several very interesting options. You can lengthen the object by a percent or by a specific amount. You may also give AutoCAD LT an overall length for a object and it will modify the object to suit that length.

Command line: lengthen, or the alias 'len'

Menu: Modify>Lengthen

Toolbar:

You can use lengthen to find the existing length of an object. Issue the command and select the object. AutoCAD LT will tell you its length.

The command in action

To try this command with the Delta option, draw a line 4 units long. You can increase or decrease it by 3 units. Issue the Lengthen command. All the options are displayed:

DElta/Percent/Total/DYnamic/<Select objects>:

If you select an object now, AutoCAD LT will simply tell you its length and then return you to the options again. You must select an option to change the object's length. Type DE for the Delta option. This will allow you to change the object's length by 3 units (-3 will decrease it, +3 will increase it). The prompt changes to:

Angle/<Enter delta length>:   type in a length and press
                                      Enter

<Select the object to change>/Undo:

Note how two of the options begin with 'D' so you have to type the first two letters to distinguish them.

Be careful as to which part of the entity you select. Click near to end you want the change to occur. Press Enter to finish the command.

Try each of the other options yourself.

Trim

How the command works

Trim allows you to clip off pieces of objects that intersect with other objects. Think of the Trim command as a pair of scissors which will cut along an edge (called a cutting edge). AutoCAD LT will ask you for a cutting edge. Once you tell it, it will want to know which objects you want to get rid of. Once you select these the command will trim them away.

Command line: trim, or the alias 'tr'

Menu: Modify>Trim

Toolbar:

If you select the wrong cutting edge just type 'u' and press Enter. AutoCAD LT will leave you in the command and you can proceed to selecting new objects.

The command in action

Issue the Trim command. Select the objects along which you want to cut or trim when you are asked:

Select cutting edges: This is actually one phrase. Read it as

Select objects: 'select the objects you want to form the cutting edge'

Select objects to trim: Select the object(s)

Press Enter to finish the command.

Trim will allow you to select several cutting edges at the same time.

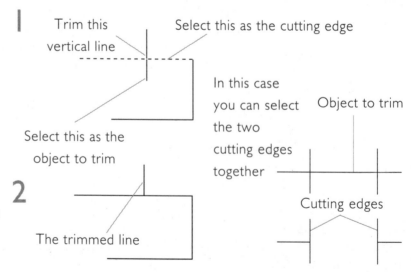

Trim this vertical line

Select this as the cutting edge

In this case you can select the two cutting edges together

Object to trim

Select this as the object to trim

The trimmed line

Cutting edges

Extend

How the command works

You can extend the length of an object to meet another object. The object you are extending to is called the boundary. You cannot extend objects which are parallel because they will never meet.

Command line: extend, or the alias 'ex'

Menu: Modify>Extend

Toolbar:

The command in action

Issue the Extend command. Select the boundary you want to extend to in the usual way when AutoCAD LT prompts:

Select boundary edges:
Select objects:

This is actually one phrase. Read it as 'select the objects you want to form the boundary edge'

Boundary edge

Line to extend

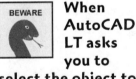

When AutoCAD LT asks you to select the object to extend, you must click on the side of the object near the boundary, otherwise AutoCAD LT will tell you there is no boundary in the other direction.

Boundary edge selected

Pickbox selecting the line to be extended

Note that the pickbox is near the end you want to extend

Chamfer

How the command works

Chamfer will join two lines by adding a third line. The easiest way to understand the command is to apply it to two lines joining at a right angle. AutoCAD LT will need to know how much of each line is to be removed (called the chamfer distance) before the third line is drawn to join the ends.

Command line: chamfer, or the alias 'cha'

Menu: Modify>Chamfer

Toolbar:

The command in action

Issue the Chamfer command. The following options are displayed:

Polyline/Distance/Angle/Trim/Method/<Select first line>:

Before you select the line check the distance by typing 'd'.

1 You must input two chamfer distances. The first one applies to the first line you pick.

2 In both these cases the chamfer distance 1 was 30 units and the second distance was 10 units.

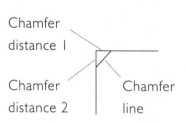

Chamfer distance 1

Chamfer distance 2

Chamfer line

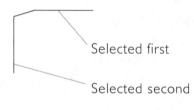

Selected first

Selected second

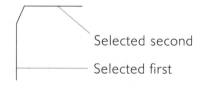
Selected second

Selected first

Fillet

How the command works

Fillet puts a curve on a sharp corner. The curve is actually an arc. AutoCAD LT will ask you for a radius for the arc. Once this is input the command finishes automatically. Issue the command again and apply the radius you input.

Command line: fillet, or the alias 'f'

Menu: Modify>Fillet

Toolbar:

The command in action

Issue the Fillet command. Type 'r' to select the radius option. Type in a value and press enter. The command will end. Right-click the mouse to call up the floating menu. Select 'Repeat Fillet' and select lines to apply the radius you entered.

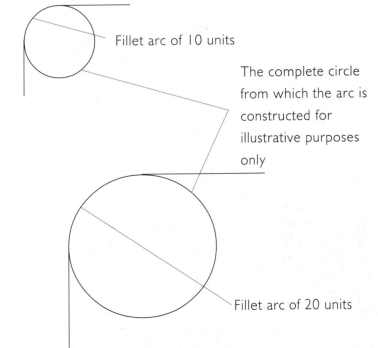

Fillet arc of 10 units

The complete circle from which the arc is constructed for illustrative purposes only

Fillet arc of 20 units

Break

HANDY TIP

When AutoCAD LT asks you to select the object, it is also asking you to select the first break point.

How the command works

Break carries out several interesting actions on an object. Take, for example, a line. AutoCAD LT allows you to break a gap in the line; it allows you to erase a section of the line. It also allows you to put an invisible break point on the line. Two points are selected on the object and AutoCAD LT will remove the section of the object between them.

Command line: break, or the alias 'br'

Menu: Modify > Break

Toolbar:

The command in action

Try this command on a line. Issue the Break command. AutoCAD LT responds with:

Select object: Pick a point on the line

Enter second point (or F for first point):   Pick a second point

HANDY TIP

If you do not want to use the first point you selected as a break point just type 'f' and Enter. AutoCAD LT will let you pick a new point.

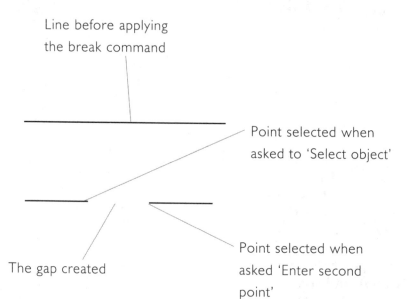

Line before applying the break command

Point selected when asked to 'Select object'

The gap created

Point selected when asked 'Enter second point'

Break – Examples in Action

Using break to erase part of the line
Pick a point on the line and then pick a point off the end of the line:

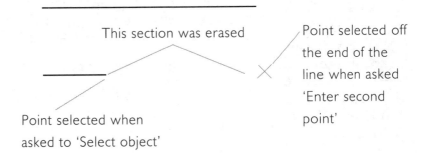

This section was erased

Point selected off the end of the line when asked 'Enter second point'

Point selected when asked to 'Select object'

Making an invisible break
Pick a point on the line. In response to 'Enter second point' type in the @ symbol. AutoCAD LT will insert an invisible break.

An invisible break is one that will not be seen when the drawing it plotted/printed.

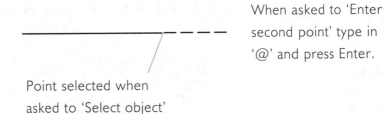

When asked to 'Enter second point' type in '@' and press Enter.

Point selected when asked to 'Select object'

You can check to see if an invisible break has occurred by using the Erase command. Part of the line up to the invisible break will highlight.

Using polar co-ordinates with break
When AutoCAD LT asks for 'Enter second point', type in a polar co-ordinate distance and angle. In the case of this horizontal line, a value like @12<0 will create a gap 12 units wide.

Arrays

How the command works

Array produces copies of objects either in rows or columns or around a central point (polar array). In the rectangular array you need to select the objects to be arrayed and tell AutoCAD LT the number of columns and rows and the distance between them. In the polar array you select a point around which the array is created.

Command line: array, or the alias 'ar'

Menu: Modify>Array

Toolbar: ⊞

The command in action

A polar array will be considered here to array a triangle. Issue the command. The Array dialogue box is displayed.

Click here for a Polar Array

Select the object to be arrayed – in this case a triangle

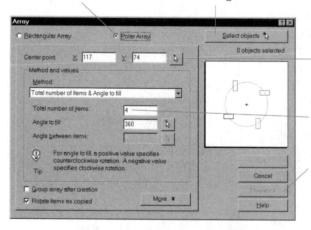

Pick the centre point of the array

Enter 24 here

Click to see a preview of the arrayed object(s)

When the preview is shown AutoCAD LT will offer to allow you to Accept or Modify the array. Selecting Modify returns you to the dialogue box.

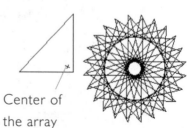

Center of the array

Text, Points and Units

In this chapter, you'll learn how to place text on a drawing. Editing of the text, including the use of the spell checker, is also treated. The old problem of selecting a text size for plotting/printing is tackled concisely on page 77. The use of the drawing object's points and the various point styles are covered in detail. And lastly, we will look at how you can control the setup and display of units in the Units Control dialogue box.

Chapter Six

Covers

Using Single Line Text

Introduction to text commands

Text is very important in precision drawings such as those produced by AutoCAD LT. Text is an object on a drawing, just as a line or a circle is an object. This implies that it is open to the same editing commands such as Scale, Move and Erase. AutoCAD LT allows you to use many different styles of text. You can also create a style yourself from the given fonts.

Text is an entity that can be scaled, moved, mirrored, etc.

Single Line Text

At times you will need to just put a line of text on the drawing for the purpose of annotation. For this you use the Single Line Text command. If you need to place several lines of text on the drawing use the Multiline Text editor.

How the command works

AutoCAD LT will ask you to click on a start point for the text. A cursor will display at that point. You then type the text and press Enter to move to the next line or Enter again to finish the command. The options available allow you to justify the text (left, right or centre) or apply a style. Once a point is selected you must supply the text height and the angle of orientation.

Command: dtext, or the alias 'dt'

Menu: Draw>Single Line Text

Pressing the spacebar inserts a space in the 'Text' option. Normally in AutoCAD LT it is the equivalent of pressing the Enter key.

The command in action

Issue the Single Line Text command. Select a start point. Enter a height. This height can be clicked with the cursor. AutoCAD LT will offer you the last height you used as the default. A rotation angle of 0 means the text is horizontal. At the prompt 'Text', type in the text you want. This is one of the few cases where pressing the spacebar will in fact put in a space and not be interpreted as Enter.

AutoCAD LT in easy steps
by Paul Whelan

Start or insertion point   Standard text font

Paragraph Text

How the command works

Use this text option to place several lines of text in a drawing. When the command is issued you will be asked to specify the corners of a box. The text you type will fill the box. AutoCAD LT opens a small word processor for you to enter and edit the text.

Command: mtext, or the alias 'mt'

Menu: Draw>Paragraph Text

Toolbar:

The command in action

Issue the Paragraph Text command. Pick a 'first' and 'opposite' corner to show AutoCAD LT where you want the text positioned. The Multiline Text Editor opens:

The current font

Click here for other fonts

Font size

Holds special characters, like the degree or diameter symbol

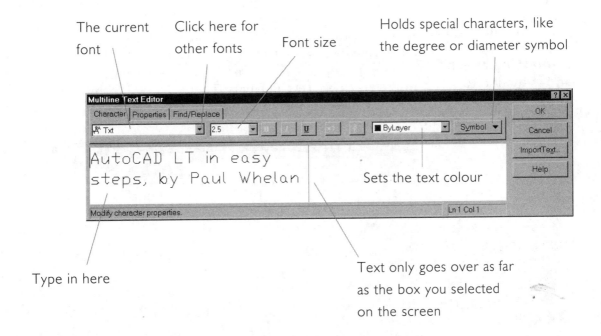

Type in here

Sets the text colour

Text only goes over as far as the box you selected on the screen

Click on OK when you have finished with the editor.

Multiline Text Editor Options

REMEMBER

The style option under the Properties tab will contain the STANDARD style only, unless you have already defined some styles yourself.

The Character, Properties and Find/Replace tabs lead into many options within the Multiline Text Editor. The Properties tab is shown below.

Positions text within the box. Select the text by dragging over it and then select the justification option

Allows you to change the width of the text box

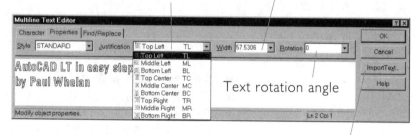

Text rotation angle

HANDY TIP

The Rich Text Format (rtf) retains the formatting of text and is available under Save As in most word processors.

Click here to import a text document written outside of AutoCAD LT

When the Import Text button is selected, the 'Open' dialogue box is displayed to allow you to look through folders for the text file. Most word processors can save files in the rtf (Rich Text Format). This is a good format to use for files which you want to import into AutoCAD LT.

BEWARE

You can only import files up to 16K in size.

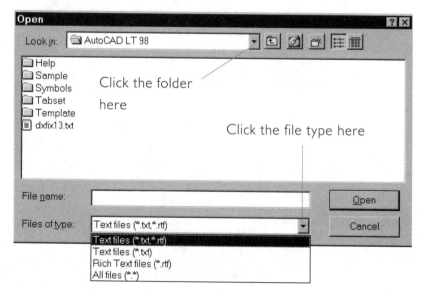

Click the folder here

Click the file type here

The Spell Checker

The spell checker can be called up by typing spell or the alias 'sp' at the command line.

The spell checker is found under the Tools drop-down menu.

Menu: Tools>Spelling

Toolbar:

The suggested word. If this is not correct, select the word from the list or type the word here

Ignore all occurrences of the word

The spell check dialogue box will only appear if there is a misspelling in the text you have selected.

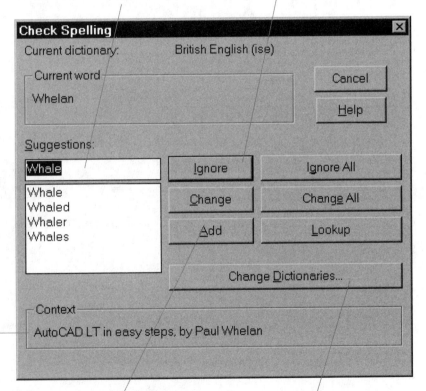

Check Spelling

Current dictionary: British English (ise)

Current word

Whelan

Cancel

Help

Suggestions:

Whale

Whale
Whaled
Whaler
Whales

Ignore   Ignore All

Change   Change All

Add   Lookup

Change Dictionaries...

Context

AutoCAD LT in easy steps, by Paul Whelan

The sentence selected on the drawing for checking

Adds the word to the dictionary so it will be recognised the next time

Offers American and British dictionaries

Editing Text

Command line: ddedit, or the alias 'ed'

Menu: Modify>Object>Text...

Icon: A∕

The Multiline Text Editor will only open if the text was originally inserted using the Paragraph Text command.

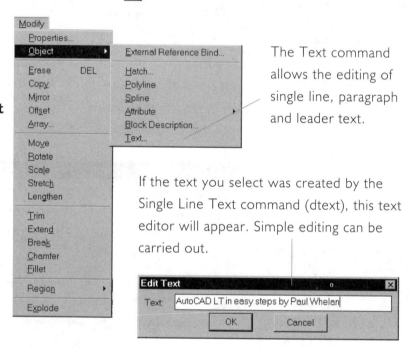

The Text command allows the editing of single line, paragraph and leader text.

If the text you select was created by the Single Line Text command (dtext), this text editor will appear. Simple editing can be carried out.

If the text you select was created by the Paragraph Text command (mtext), the Multiline Text Editor will open with the selected text. This text can then be modified in the usual way, including changing font or style, etc.

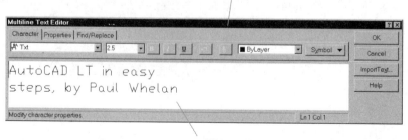

The selected text is loaded into the editor

Text Size and Plotting/Printing

If you are unsure at what scale the drawing will be printed, input the text as though the plot will be 1:100. Changing the text size to 1:25, or 1:250 is then easy.

When you are selecting text height for a drawing, you must try and keep in mind the scale that the drawing will eventually be plotted at. Because text is often the only object on a drawing that does not represent something in the real world, it is not placed on the drawing in real world size.

Text size on a plotted drawing

To find out the size the text will be on the printed drawing you must divide the text height by the plot scale. For example:

Text height input = 500mm

Drawing plotted = 1:100

The phrase 'plot scale' is the scale the drawing is printed at. If you print at 1:50, then 50 is the plot scale.

Text height on the plotted drawing is 500/100 = 5mm

And vice versa, if the text must be 8mm high on a drawing at 1:250, the calculation is:

8*250 = 2000mm

Some other examples:

- 4mm text is input as 400mm on a 1:100 plot.
- 5mm text is input as 250mm on a 1:50 plot.
- 6mm text is input as 150mm on a 1:25 plot.

Multiply the height you want the text to be on the printed drawing by the scale factor it is printed at, to find out what size you enter the text at.

Text for signs on a drawing will be shown in real world size and consequently must be input in real world size just as any other object in the drawing.

Text Styles

Introduction

AutoCAD LT comes with many text fonts. Each one of these fonts can be modified by, say, changing the angle it slopes at, or its thickness, etc. These changes constitute a style. All the fonts available in AutoCAD LT have a single predefined style called STANDARD.

How the command works

AutoCAD LT will offer you the current style. You can edit this or create a new style. If you create a new style you must give it a name. A style can be deleted at any time.

Command line: ddstyle

Menu: Format>Text Style

The command in action

Issue the Text Style command. Fill in the Text Style dialogue box – see page 79 opposite.

A text style is a set of changes made to a font.

This is the default
AutoCAD LT style

AutoCAD LT in easy steps by Paul Whelan

The standard style modified by setting
the obliquing angle to 30 degrees

AutoCAD LT in easy steps by Paul Whelan

The standard font was used
running backwards in this style

nɒləAW luɒꟼ ʏd ꙅqɘƚꙅ ʏꙅɒɘ ni T⅃ ᗡAↃoƚuA

Text Style Dialogue Box

 REMEMBER

The point you select to start the text on the drawing is the 'insertion point'.

Allows you to rename the current style

Allows you to delete the current style

Click New to create a new style

The current style

To see the other fonts a style may be based on, click the down-arrow

Text runs upside down from the insertion point

Text runs backwards from the insertion point

Text runs vertical from the insertion point

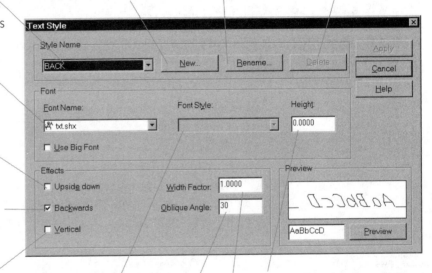

Basic fonts style

Angle of slope of each letter

Width of each letter

If you enter a height other than 0 you will not be asked for height input when you use the dtext or mtext commands.

BEWARE

If you enter a text height in this dialogue box then the style will always be set to that height.

Points

If you have layers set up for the drawing, it's a good idea to place the points on a separate layer. This will allow you to make them invisible without regenerating the complete drawing.

Introduction

A point is an object. It can be placed in the drawing as a marker to show boundaries or elevation points. A point can be made invisible so that it does not plot or print. You can object snap to a point using the mode Node.

How the command works

There are 20 basic symbols used to represent a point. Simply click on a position on the screen for the point. AutoCAD LT uses the default point shape and size or the last setting used. To change these settings see the Point Style dialogue box.

Command line: point, or the alias 'po'

Menu: Draw>Point>Single Point

Toolbar:

The Object Snap Node icon:

The command in action

Issue the Point command. Select the position for the point in the usual way. If you cannot see the point, then switch the grid off if you have it displayed. If you still cannot see it, change the Point Style.

The system variables PDMODE and PDSIZE can be used to change the size and appearance of the points.

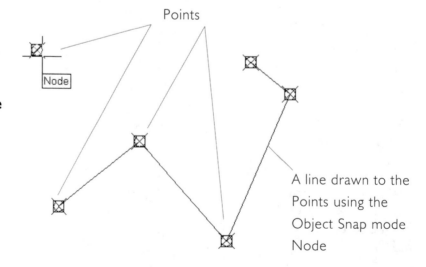

Points

Node

A line drawn to the Points using the Object Snap mode Node

Point Style

You can only use one point style at a time.

How the command works

Select a point from the library. This will become the current style. You can only use one point style at a time in a drawing. To see the effect of selecting a new point style you must type Regen at the command line and press Enter.

Command line: ddptype

Menu: Format>Point Style

The command in action

Issue the Point Style command. The Point Style dialogue box is displayed. Select a point by clicking on it and selecting OK.

The default point is a dot

The invisible point: the points remain on the drawing but are rendered invisible

If the drawing is very large, then the Regen command may take a while to regenerate the whole drawing.

Points can be displayed as a percentage of the overall screen size

Click here to set the point size to use the units of the drawing

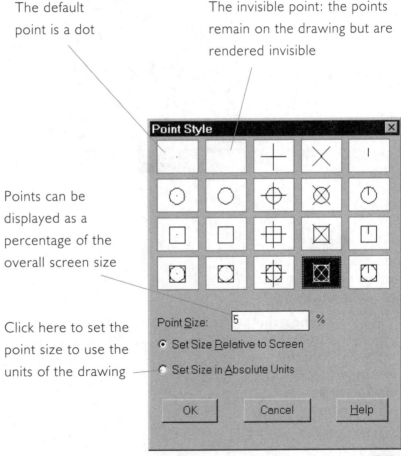

Controlling the Drawing Units

HANDY TIP

The units can be changed at any time during the drawing process.

How the command works
The units control dialogue box allows you to change the type of drawing units and their precision.

Command line: ddunits

Menu: Format>Units

The command in action
Issue the Units command. The Units Control dialogue box is displayed.

Select the drawing units here

Select the method for angle measurement here

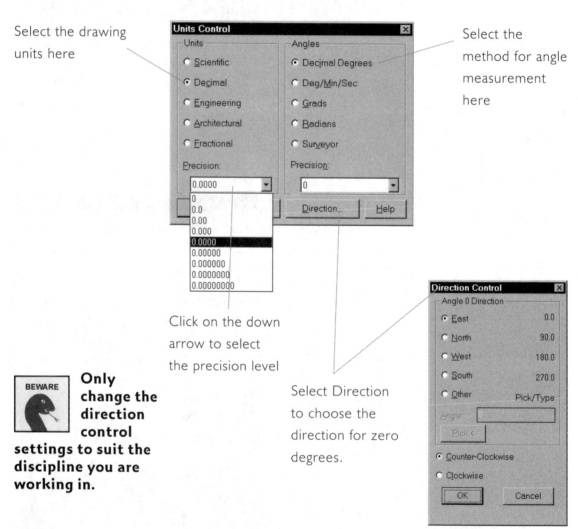

Click on the down arrow to select the precision level

Select Direction to choose the direction for zero degrees.

BEWARE

Only change the direction control settings to suit the discipline you are working in.

Working with Layers

In this chapter you will learn to use layers. Layers are used to control the display of objects; they also help directly in the drawing and editing procedures by enabling you to assign colours and linetypes to them.

Chapter Seven

Covers

Layers

Introduction

An AutoCAD LT drawing can be constructed over several layers. A layer is like a transparent sheet of paper which holds drawing objects. For example, a drawing of the plans of a house could be constructed as follows: the walls would occupy a layer called 'walls', the doors and windows would be placed on a layer called 'fittings', etc. When a drawing is structured in this way you have control over numerous aspects of the work.

A layer can be assigned a linetype and a colour.

AutoCAD LT supplies you with one default layer named o. Any other layers must be created by the you, the user, although you can assign as many layers as you like to a drawing. A layer is not limited in the number of objects it can hold. Each layer must have its own distinct name.

Layers always lie directly under each other and cannot be moved. Layers can be made visible or invisible, and can be assigned a colour or a linetype so that each object drawn on the layer will be in the specified colour and linetype.

Often the colour of a linetype is used to indicate the thickness of a line. Even if the printer/plotter device you use is monochrome, assigning colours to layers can be very important.

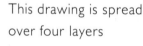

This drawing is spread over four layers

Main structure of the drawing on this layer

If you draw something on the wrong layer, AutoCAD LT will allow you to place it back on the correct layer.

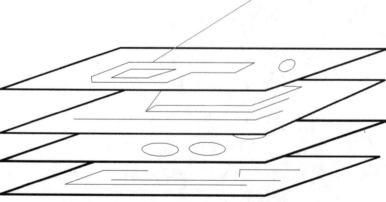

Setting up a New Layer

 HANDY TIP

Give layers names that describe what they contain.

Here we will set up two layers called Walls and Fittings. To create a new layer, first issue the Layer command:

Command line: layer, or the alias 'la'

Menu: Format>Layer

Icon:

| In the Layer & Linetype Properties dialogue box, click on New.

The current layer – the one you are working on – is shown as 0 here.

Displays the linetype in use by a layer

Tab for setting up the layers

Tab for setting up linetypes

Holds the names of all the layers setup for this drawing

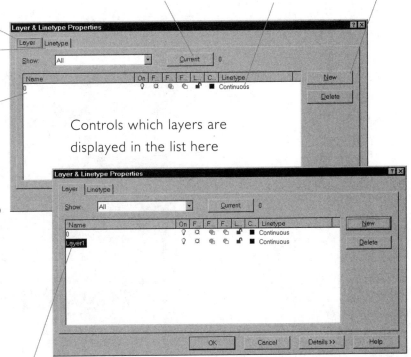

Controls which layers are displayed in the list here

 BEWARE

There is a special relationship between blocks and layers (see Chapter Eight).

 HANDY TIP

You can rename a layer by highlighting its name and pressing the F2 function key.

2 Type in your Layer I named Walls and press Enter.

3 Click on New again, type in the layer name 'Fittings' and press Enter. Both layers are now set up.

Assigning a Colour to a Layer

Assigning a colour to a layer means that everything drawn on that layer will take on that colour.

1 In the Layer & Linetype Properties dialogue box, click on the colour box for the Walls layer.

These are the layers you set up

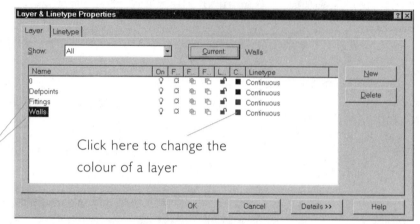

Click here to change the colour of a layer

2 Click on the colour red for the Walls layer in the Select Colour dialogue box.

Click on red and then OK

To assign the same colour to several layers at once, just hold the Ctrl key and click on the name of each layer. They will all be highlighted. Then click on the colour. This action opens the Select Colour dialogue box.

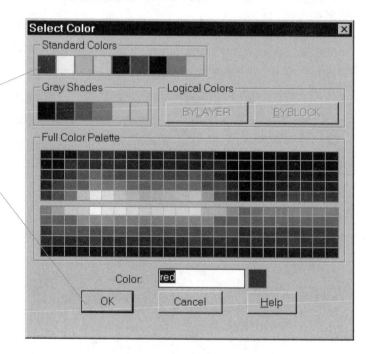

3 Assign the colour green to the layer Fittings.

Making a Layer Current

A layer must be current before you can draw on it. To make the layer 'Walls' current, carry out the following easy steps:

1 Click on the layer name in the Layer & Linetype Properties dialogue box, then click on the Current button.

2 Click OK to return to the drawing editor.

3 The Object Properties toolbar at the top of the screen (see below) will show the name of the current layer and its colour. Try drawing something. It will appear in red.

Layers icon   Current layer and colour

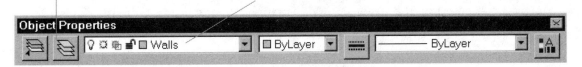

Alternatively, to make a layer current from within the drawing editor:

To follow these examples set up two layers: a 'Walls' layer with the colour red and a 'Fittings' layer in green.

1 Click here.

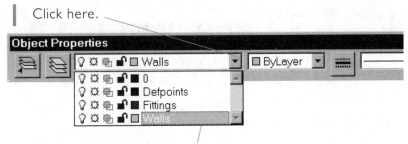

2 Click here near the layer name.

3 Click out on the drawing editor anywhere.

Draw an object such as a line or circle and it will take on the colour property of the layer selected.

Now make the 'Fittings' layer current and draw an object on it. It should appear in green.

Making Layers Visible or Invisible

Why control the visibility of layers?

AutoCAD LT allows you to switch a layer 'off' (invisible) or 'on' (visible).

A layer which is invisible is not printed. Sensitive information on a drawing can be placed on a separate layer and made invisible.

Complex drawings may become cluttered, which can make it difficult to select objects for editing or drawing. This clutter may be reduced by making a layer invisible if you are not working on it. When a layer is made invisible, the objects drawn on it disappear from the screen, but they still exist and are part of the drawing. Layers which are invisible are not printed. This has the advantage of allowing you to print selected layers of a drawing.

For example, a builder of a house may not be interested in the furnishings which an interior designer has placed on the drawing. The furnishings layer can be made invisible and the drawing then plotted for the builder.

Several layers can be made invisible if required. The icon for visible is a glowing light bulb. Invisibility is shown by a dull light bulb. To make a layer visible or invisible:

A yellow light bulb means the layer is on or visible.

| Click here.

2 Click here on the light bulb.

3 Click out on the drawing editor anywhere.

It is advisable not to switch off the current layer.

Generally, there is no sense in making the layer you are working on (the current layer) invisible. If you attempt to switch it off, AutoCAD LT will warn you.

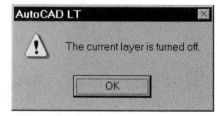

Freezing and Thawing Layers

REMEMBER

A layer which is frozen cannot be made current.

When a drawing is regenerated (the Regen command) AutoCAD LT reconstructs the complete drawing from scratch. This may take a considerable length of time on a complex drawing. To save regeneration time you can freeze a layer. A layer which is frozen is not regenerated. Text is slow to regenerate, so you could place the text on a separate layer and freeze it.

To return a frozen layer to its normal condition you thaw it. A thawed layer is visible and will regenerate.

To freeze a layer

HANDY TIP

You can change the properties of several layers at the one time by just clicking on them.

Click here.

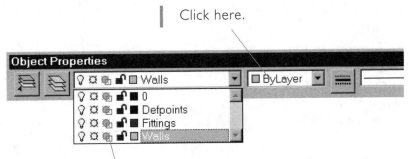

2 Click here on the 'cloudy' sun to freeze.

3 Click out on the drawing editor anywhere.

HANDY TIP

A layer which is frozen is also invisible.

To thaw a layer

Click here.

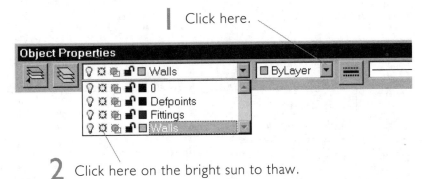

2 Click here on the bright sun to thaw.

3 Click out on the drawing editor anywhere.

Freezing and Viewports

REMEMBER

Freeze layers which you will not be using for a long time, and/or which contain a lot of text or hatching.

Open the Layer & Linetype Properties dialogue box (Format>Layer). Some of the column headings in the dialogue box begin 'F...'. Pull these back to reveal the full heading(s) by following the steps:

1 Move the cursor to here. It will turn to a vertical bar with opposing arrows.

HANDY TIP

A viewport is a window set up within AutoCAD LT to allow two or more views of the same drawing (see page 180 for more on *Viewports*).

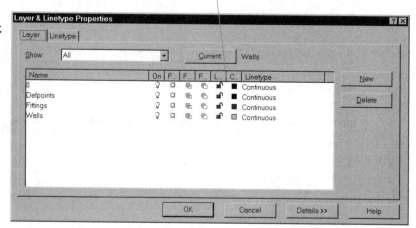

BEWARE

When you thaw a layer it will regenerate.

2 Depress the left mouse button and drag to the right.

3 The full heading becomes visible.

This refers to tiled viewports in model space

This option works only in untiled or floating viewports

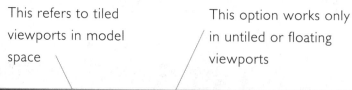

Freeze in All Viewports	Freeze in Current Viewport	Freeze in New Viewports

REMEMBER

When you are using the default drawing editor, you are working in a single tiled viewport in model space.

This is useful if you are working in floating viewports. As you create new viewports the selected layers will automatically be frozen

Lock, Delete and Details

Lock/Unlock
A layer can be locked. A locked layer cannot be edited, but objects on a locked layer may be used to help edit an unlocked layer. For example, you can trim a line on an unlocked layer back to a line on a locked layer. You cannot trim the line on the locked layer.

How to lock/unlock a layer

Lock a layer if someone else is working on the drawing and you want to 'remind' them not to change anything on that particular layer.

Click here.

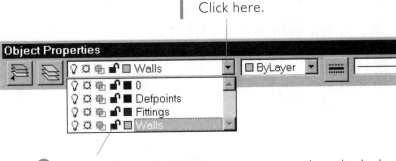

2 Click here on the lock icon to open or close the lock

3 Click out on the drawing editor anywhere

Delete
A layer may be deleted if it is unreferenced in any way. Basically this means that there must be no objects on it; it cannot be the default layer o; it cannot be the 'defpoints' layer (created by AutoCAD LT when you start dimensioning objects); it cannot be part of a block or an xref.

If you're working with a standard set of layers, it is advisable not to delete any layers unless you talk to the project manager.

Details
This button provides a summary (not more details!) of the selected layer.

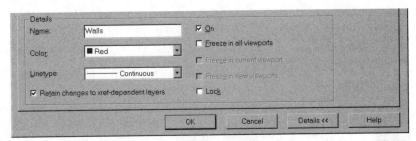

Linetypes

Introduction
The default linetype in AutoCAD LT is continuous. Everything you draw is shown with a continuous linetype. To draw with a dashed or dotted (or other) linetype you need to look in the two libraries of linetypes supplied. The libraries are found in the files *aclt.lin* and *acltiso.lin*.

BEWARE

If the template drawing you use is based on the acltiso template, you should use the acltiso.lin library.

How to access a linetype
The steps for using a linetype are: firstly the linetype must be loaded into AutoCAD LT from a library; secondly it must be set to being current.

How to use a linetype
Once a linetype is loaded into AutoCAD LT you are ready to use it by making it current. That can be done in one of the following ways:

- Assign it to a layer – this is called the Bylayer method

- Assign it to a block – this is called the Byblock method

- Assign it to an object – to do this you just make the linetype current and draw

HANDY TIP

If you know how to set up your own template drawings, then load all the linetypes you frequently use into the template so that they are easily available.

Linetype name   Visual description

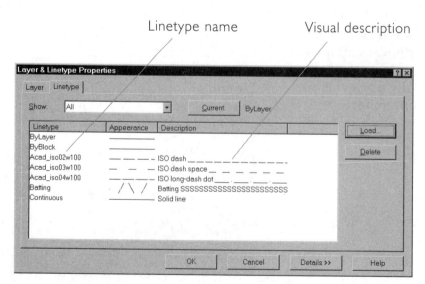

How to Load a Linetype

REMEMBER

A linetype has to be loaded before it can be used.

1 In the Object Properties toolbar pick the linetype icon or type Linetype at the command line.

2 Click on Load.

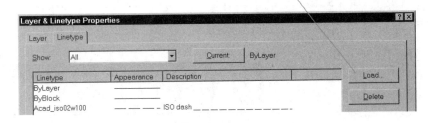

HANDY TIP

You can create your own linetypes if there are none that suit you in the aclt or acltiso libraries.

3 Make sure acltiso.lin is in this box – click on File if it's missing and select it from the library list.

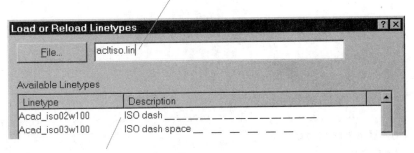

HANDY TIP

A linetype only has to be loaded once during the time you work on a file. It is saved with the file and is available the next time you open the drawing.

4 Click on the linetype you want to load – try ISO dash.

5 Click on OK.

6 The linetype is now loaded and added to the list in the Layer & Linetype Properties dialogue box.

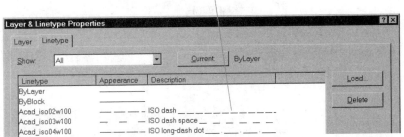

Linetypes – ßyLayer

Linetypes and layers – ßyLayer

You can associate a linetype with a layer so that the linetype automatically becomes current when the layer is current. To do this follow the steps:

If the LTScale setting is not correct, the linetype may still look continuous.

1 Open the Layer & Linetype Properties dialogue box by clicking on the icon 🗇 or Format>Layers.

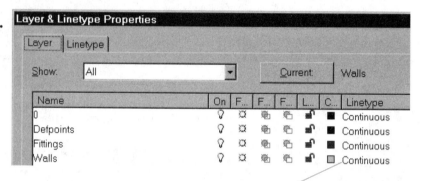

There are several other ways to carry out the procedures here. You may discover a more suitable way.

2 In the Layer & Linetype Properties dialogue box click on Continuous under Linetype.

3 The Select Linetype dialogue box opens. Select the linetype you want and click on OK. If it is not listed, click on Load and follow the procedure for loading a linetype.

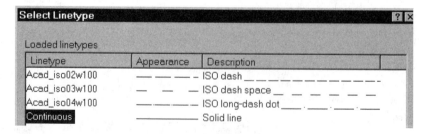

4 To see how successful you were, make the layer current and draw a line or two on it.

5 If the lines still seem continuous, see Scaling Linetypes (page 98).

Linetypes by Object

Setting a linetype current

It is possible to draw different objects on the same layer with different linetypes. To do this follow the steps below.

1 Open the Layer & Linetype Properties dialogue box by clicking on the icon or Format>Layers.

2 Click on the Linetype tab.

3 Highlight the linetype you want to use.

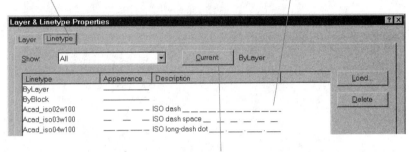

<table>
<tr><td colspan="4">Layer & Linetype Properties</td></tr>
</table>

4 Click on current.

AutoCAD LT does not assign a thickness to any linetype. For plotting purposes you can use the colour option by assigning a colour to a pen of a particular width. See *Plotting Line Thicknesses* on page 188.

5 Click on OK. The objects you now draw will use the current linetype.

The Show linetype option

The linetypes displayed can be filtered in ways similar to that of the layers.

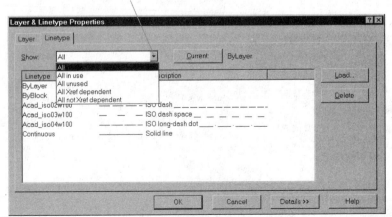

Making a Layer Current by Object

To draw on a layer you need to make it current first. If you have objects drawn on a layer already, and if you wish to make that layer current then use the icon:

In the illustration below, the circle and the line are on different layers. The line is on the current layer, but to make the layer the circle is on current, carry out the following steps:

| Click on the icon.

2 Click on the circle.

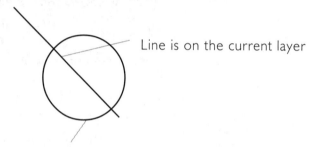

Line is on the current layer

The layer the circle is on is made current by selecting it

How to Unlock a Layer

| Click on the layers icon.

2 Click on the 'Layer' tab and select the layer name you want to unlock.

3 Click on 'Details >>' at the bottom of the dialogue box.

4 Remove the tick from the 'Lock' box.

HANDY TIP

You can also lock/ unlock a layer using the Object Properties toolbar (see page 91). Try it!

Moving Objects to a Different Layer

If you draw objects on the wrong layer, AutoCAD LT allows you to place them on the correct layer without redrawing them. Each object in a drawing has properties associated with it. The colour of an object or the layer it is on are examples of properties.

To change the layer an object is on you use the Change Properties command.

How the command works

Select the object you want to move to a new layer and then select the layer:

Command line: ddchprop

Menu: Modify>Properties...

The command in action

The dialogue box which is displayed at step 2 may differ from that shown. In the illustration on this page an xref was selected, hence AutoCAD LT displayed the Modify External Reference dialogue box.

1 Issue the command and select the object(s) you want to move to a different layer.

2 Press Enter when you have finished selecting the object(s). The Change Properties dialogue box is displayed.

3 Click on the Layer button and select the layer you want from the list. Click OK and OK again to see the change.

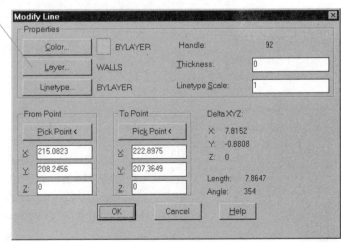

Scaling Linetypes – Ltscale

The scale of a linetype (or ltscale) refers to the spacing of the elements that make up the linetype. For example, the dashes in a linetype may be 4 units long and the spaces may be 2 units. These spacings can be scaled up or down from the default settings. The default setting is a scale of 1. To change the ltscale on a dashed linetype carry out the following steps:

The examples here use the line object, but the same explanation applies for any object drawn in a particular linetype.

1 From the Format menu select Linetype...

2 The Layer & Linetype Properties dialogue box is displayed.

3 Click on the linetype you want to readjust.

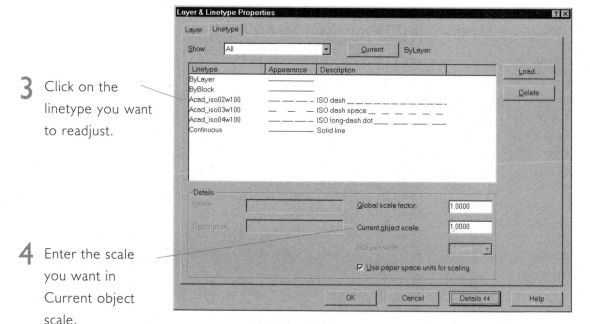

4 Enter the scale you want in Current object scale.

5 Click OK and draw a line. The new scale setting will apply.

To change the linetype scale of a line already drawn, you must use the Modify>Properties menu. Once the line is selected, the Modify Line dialogue box appears and contains the option to change the scale.

Blocks and Xrefs

Blocks are formed by grouping objects together. You will learn to insert blocks and drawings into other drawings. The difference between blocks and xrefs is explained, and then xrefs are treated in full. Finally, the Content Explorer is used to organise the blocks and xrefs.

Covers

Chapter Eight

What is a Block?

BEWARE

Once a block is made, you need a special procedure to edit it. See the explode command on page 105.

A block is an object or group of objects which are gathered together and given a name. Once the group of objects has a name you can use it in the drawing as many time as you like. You can also use it in drawings other than the one it was created in.

You can build up your own library of blocks or purchase third party libraries. Typical examples of blocks are doors and windows, or electrical components such as switches and transistors.

A complete drawing can be treated as a block. For example you could draw a room and later add it into a separate drawing of a house.

A block has an insertion point. This is the point that it is picked up at for insertion into a drawing.

HANDY TIP

Blocks should be drawn at real world size.

Three examples of blocks

1. A block of a door

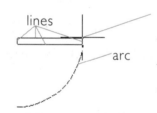

lines

Possible insertion point

arc

The arc and lines are grouped together and given a name. This is called a block

2. A block of a man

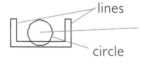

lines

Possible insertion point

circle

HANDY TIP

Keep all the blocks you make in a separate folder from the drawings.

3. A block of a barge

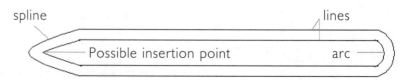

spline

lines

Possible insertion point

arc

Blocks and Layers

A block can be created on a single layer or spread over several layers. The layers a block is created on can affect the performance of the blocks when it's used in a drawing at a later stage.

Layer O blocks

Layer o is quite special. Any block created on layer o will position itself on the current layer when it is placed in a drawing. The block will then take on the properties of that layer.

HANDY TIP

If a block is spread over several layers, it will bring those layers into a drawing when it is inserted.

Here is an example: imagine a drawing with just two layers – layer o (white) and layer Walls (red). If a block is created wholly on layer o it will be white in colour. If the user then makes layer Walls (red) current and proceeds to insert the block into the drawing, the block will sit into the layer Walls and appear red in colour.

Lastly, when this block is exploded for editing, it will fall back down to layer o and take on the properties of that layer.

Blocks created on layers other than O

If a block is created on several layers other than layer o, it will carry those layers and their properties around with it into whatever drawing it is inserted.

REMEMBER

Layer O blocks have the special property of always inserting onto the current layer when placed into a drawing.

Here is an example: imagine a block is created from objects on two layers – Walls (red) and Windows (yellow). If this block is inserted into a drawing that does not contain those layers, then the layers will be automatically created by the block as it is inserted. The layers will have the same properties as the original two layers – red and yellow. This will occur even if the current layer at the time of insertion is layer o.

If this block is exploded for editing, the objects of the block will fall back to their original layers.

How to Make a Block

Overall view

- Draw the objects that make up the block.

- Give a name to the block.

- Decide on where the insertion point should be. This is important because you can insert the block into a drawing using object snap.

- Group the objects together.

BEWARE **The example block being created here can only be inserted into the drawing it was created in.**

Follow these easy steps:

1 Draw the door.

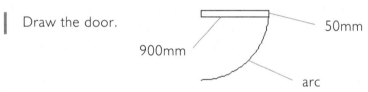

900mm

50mm

arc

2 Click on Draw.

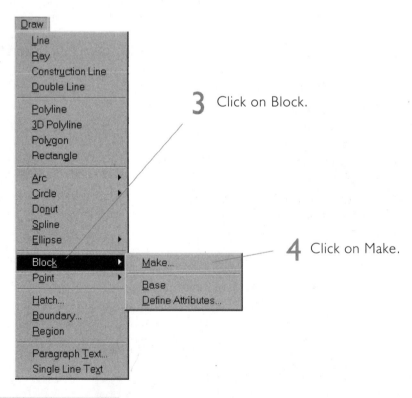

3 Click on Block.

4 Click on Make.

...cont'd

5 The following dialogue box appears.

6 Click on the Internal block button.

7 Type 'Door1'.

8 Click on Select objects. AutoCAD LT hides the dialogue box. Pull a selection window around the door and press Enter. This dialogue box will return.

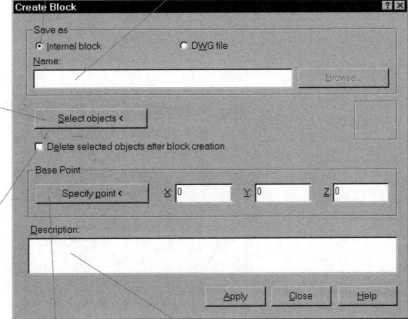

9 Leave this blank.

If an error message tells you the block name is incorrect, try removing spaces from the name.

10 Click here and then pick an insertion point on the drawing of the door. Use object snap.

11 Type a description in here such as 'This is my first block'.

12 Click on Apply.

13 Click on Close.

How to Insert a Block

This block can only be inserted into the drawing it was created in.

Once the block has been created, you may insert it into the drawing. Try this now using the block 'Door1':

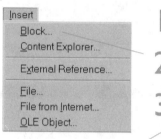

1 Click on the Insert menu.

2 Click on Block...

3 The Insert dialogue box will appear.

4 Click on Block...

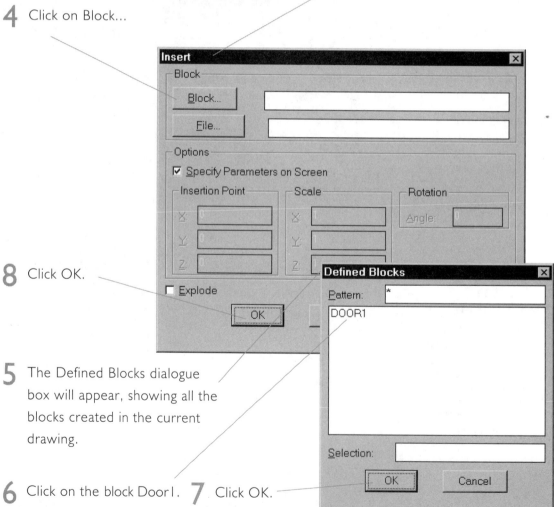

8 Click OK.

5 The Defined Blocks dialogue box will appear, showing all the blocks created in the current drawing.

6 Click on the block Door1.   7 Click OK.

...cont'd

There is a close relationship between blocks and layers. Make sure you understand layers before you create a library of blocks.

Step 11: if you move the cursor at this step you will see the effect of scaling on the X and Y axis.

If you don't have the time to master layers before working on blocks, just make sure that you use the default layer O when creating the blocks.

9   At this point you are returned to the drawing with the block attached to the cross-hairs at the insertion point you defined.

10   Move the block into position on the screen. The command line asks for the Insertion point. Click on a point on the drawing to show where you want to place the block.

11   AutoCAD LT now wants to know if you would like to scale the block on the X axis. Press Enter to accept the default value of 1 (for no scaling).

12   AutoCAD LT next wants to know if you would like to scale the block on the Y axis. Press Enter to accept the default value of 1 (for no scaling).

13   The command line wants to know if you would like to rotate the block. You could type in an angle and press Enter or just press Enter to accept the default of 0.

14   The block is now locked into position in the drawing.

This block will behave as one object when you try to edit it. Try the Move command on it, for example. The moment you select it, it will appear as a single entity.

Exploding a block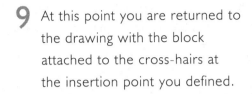

To edit or change some detail with the block you need to Explode it. Any modifications made to the exploded block do not affect the original block which you defined.

Placing One Drawing into Another

The inserted drawing will behave like a block.

Any AutoCAD LT drawing can be placed into another AutoCAD LT drawing. In the Block Insert dialogue box you select File instead of Block.

Only insert a finished drawing, otherwise you will have to explode it for editing. This could cause problems unless you are highly skilled with AutoCAD LT.

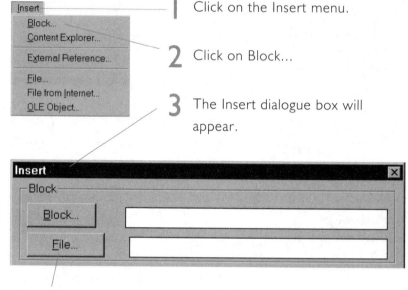

1 Click on the Insert menu.

2 Click on Block...

3 The Insert dialogue box will appear.

4 Click on File.

5 Select Drawing File dialogue box and look for the file here.

Visual preview of the highlighted drawing

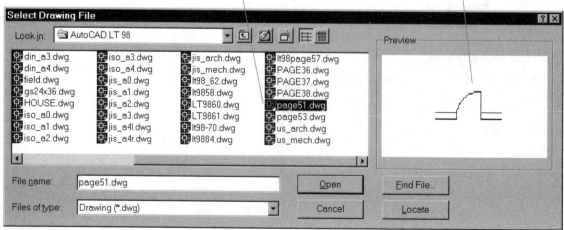

...cont'd

If you cannot find the file, then you may need to develop your skill in looking through folders. See 'Windows 95/98 in easy steps'.

6 Click on Open when you have found the file. This will return you to the Insert dialogue box. The path to the drawing file is now shown in the box.

7 Click OK to proceed with the insertion of the file. All files will have a base point of 0,0 (attached to the cross-hairs).

8 Pick an insertion point (or type a co-ordinate).

9 AutoCAD LT will ask the usual questions about scaling on the X and Y axis and the rotation angle.

How to Change the Base Point

The default base point for a drawing is o,o. To change this do the following.

HANDY TIP

If you insert a drawing and you cannot see the whole extent of it, try typing Z for zoom and Enter, and then E for extents and Enter.

1 Open the drawing.

2 Click on the Draw menu. Select Block and then click on Base.

3 AutoCAD LT will ask you to pick a new base point. Use object snap or an absolute co-ordinate if you like.

Draw
Line
Ray
Construction Line
Double Line

Polyline
3D Polyline
Polygon
Rectangle

Arc ▶
Circle ▶
Donut
Spline
Ellipse ▶

Block ▶   Make...
Point ▶

Hatch...
Boundary...
Region

Base
Define Attributes...

When you insert the drawing file it will be attached to the cross-hairs at this point.

How to Use a Block in any Drawing

If a block is converted into a drawing file then you can use it in any other drawing created by AutoCAD LT.

1 Click on Block from the Draw drop-down menu.

2 Click on Make from the cascading menu.

3 Click on the DWG file button.

4 Type in a name for the block.

The Browse option can be used to look for a folder

BEWARE

If the block was originally created as an internal block, then carry out the same procedure again with the dot in DWG file (step 3).

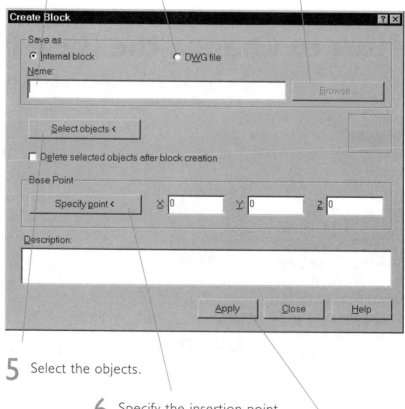

Create Block

Save as
  ⦿ Internal block   ○ DWG file
  Name:
  [   ]   Browse...

  Select objects <

  ☐ Delete selected objects after block creation

  Base Point
  Specify point <   X: 0   Y: 0   Z: 0

  Description:
  [   ]

  Apply   Close   Help

5 Select the objects.

6 Specify the insertion point.

7 Click on Apply.

External References – Xrefs

External references (or xrefs) allow you to link two or more drawings together. Below are three separate drawings:

Separate drawing file of a ball 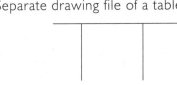 Separate drawing file of a chair

Separate drawing file of a table

An xref is very different from a block. A block becomes part of the drawing it is inserted into; an external referenced file does not.

The drawing of the table could make reference to the ball and chair drawings to produce the following drawing.

In this case the table is the *master* drawing which has made reference to two external drawings – the chair and the ball. The ball and chair drawings are not inserted into the master drawing of the table (as a block could be), but instead are *attached* to the table drawing.

The Xref command will allow you to attach drawings to a master drawing.

The drawing which references other drawings is called the 'master' file.

If the drawing file of the chair is changed in any way, then the chair in the master drawing will change also. This is better than if the chair was inserted as a block, because if the block drawing was changed, then the change would not be seen in the master drawing.

A block becomes part of the drawing it was inserted into: an external reference always remains a separate drawing.

How to Use Xrefs

To follow this section on xrefs you should create three simple drawings – of the chair, table and ball – and name them accordingly. The ball is a simple circle while the table and chair are constructed from lines. Create each of the images on a sheet of 420mm by 297 mm. Once you have done this open the drawing of the table. You will then attach the drawing of the ball by making an xref to it.

Attaching the Xref files – ball and chair

Issue the Xref command by either typing xref at the command line and pressing Enter or from the Insert toolbar select 🗋. The drop-down menu option is shown here:

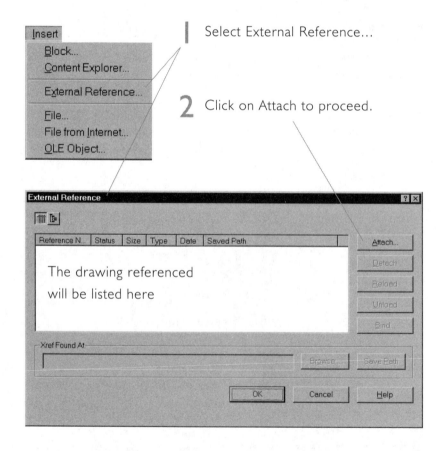

Select External Reference...

Click on Attach to proceed.

...cont'd

3 From the Select file to attach dialogue box, highlight the file you want. Check the Preview to see if it is the correct file. Then click Open.

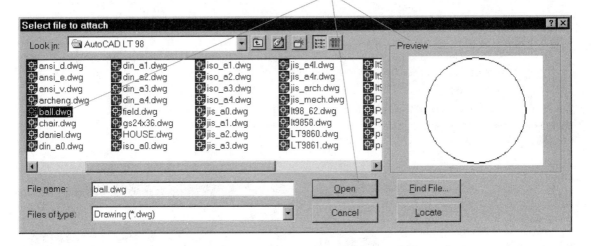

4 The Attach Xref dialogue box will confirm the selection. Click OK to continue.

Keep the names of files used in xrefs as short as possible.

Make sure the dot is in here

You may scale the drawing. In this example leave it unscaled (that is 1)

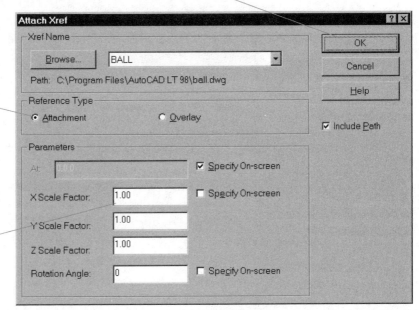

...cont'd

5 The drawing will appear attached to the cross-hairs. Position it on the table.

6 Issue the External Reference command again.

REMEMBER

An xref file is not part of the drawing it is attached to.

7 Click on Attach in the dialogue box.

8 Click on Browse.

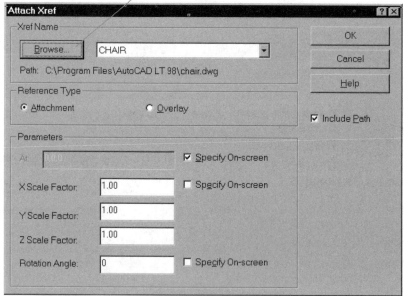

9 Select the Chair file and click on Open, and then on OK and position the chair in the drawing.

10 The files are attached. Save the drawing.

The Value of Xrefs

An xref will update automatically in the drawing it is attached to.

The value of xrefs will now be illustrated.

1 Open the drawing of the chair and edit it so that it looks like this:

2 Now save the chair and open the drawing of the ball. Edit it to look like this:

3 Save the ball drawing and open the table drawing. It should look like this:

A block becomes part of the drawing it is inserted into. Blocks will not update when they are modified.

The edits to the attached drawing are reflected in the master drawing. This occurs because the xrefs are not saved with the table drawing. Only the link to the attachments is saved. Each time the master drawing of the table is open it checks what is in the attached drawings: any changes made to them are automatically displayed.

The value of this can be seen on large projects. A master drawing can contain references to other drawings. Each of the attached drawings can be as complex as you like and can be created by different individuals on a network. As work proceeds, the master drawing will always show the latest state of the drawings.

A drawing can have any number of xrefs.

Working with Xrefs

A drawing which has an external reference must always have access to the referenced drawing while it is attached. This means that you cannot move the master drawing or the xrefs to another folder. The illustration below shows four folders: folder 1 contains the master drawing with xrefs in folders 2, 3 and 4. If the xref in folder 2 is moved to folder 3, then the master drawing will not be able to find it.

Try and keep the master drawing and its xrefs in the same folder.

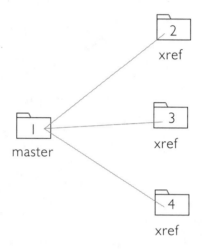

A master drawing will always look for its external references each time the drawing is opened.

This can lead to problems if a large number of xrefs are being used. A good tip for this kind of work is to keep the master drawing and all its external references in one folder. It is then easy to move the master drawing and its xrefs, particularly if you want to send the drawing to someone else to complete.

When a project is finished you can bind the xrefs into the master drawing so that they behave like blocks: they become part of the drawing and do not update automatically. The master drawing will not look for them again.

Do not move the location of an xref. If you do, the master drawing will not be able to find it.

Detaching an Xref

You may decide that an xref is no longer required in a drawing. Using the Erase command will not remove the xref. It will erase the image on the screen but when you open the master drawing again the xref will re appear. To remove any reference to the xref you must *detach* it as follows:

REMEMBER

You must detach an xref if you want to remove it from the drawing.

1 From the Insert menu click on External Reference.

2 In the External Reference dialogue box, highlight the xref you want to detach.

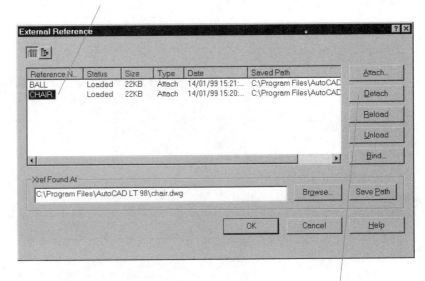

BEWARE

If you use the Erase command on an xref, it will reappear in the drawing the next time you open it.

3 Click on Detach and click OK to return to the drawing. The xref you choose will have been removed.

You must Attach the drawing file again if you want to use it as an xref.

Binding an Xref

Once a drawing is finished you might like to bind the external references into the master drawing. This will ensure that the master drawing will not look for the xrefs again. The xrefs become part of the drawing and are stored as part of the master drawing file. This allows you to send the finished drawing to other people. To bind the chair created on pages 109–110, follow the steps below.

A bound xref is not updated.

1   Open the master drawing. Click on Insert > External Reference...

2   The External Reference dialogue box lists the drawings already attached to the master drawing. Select the file you want to bind by highlighting it and then click on Bind.

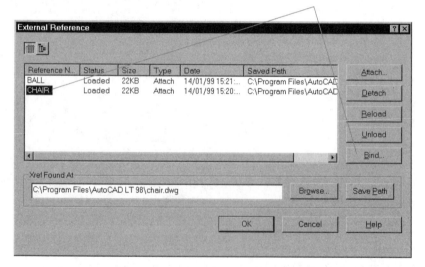

Keeps the xref image in the drawing with separate layers

3   Two options are presented in the Bind Xrefs box: Bind and Insert.

Keeps the xref as if it were inserted as a block, and so merging it with the master drawing

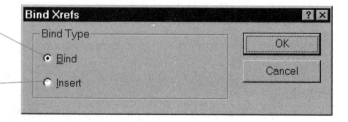

Other Xref Options

Unload

Unload removes the xref from being displayed on the screen, although it still remains attached to the drawing. You might Unload if the drawing screen is cluttered and the xref is not needed at the time of editing.

Reload

Remember where the xrefs are in a drawing if you unload them, otherwise you may draw something in the position they occupy.

Reload is used to force AutoCAD LT to re-display the xref again. This can be used if the Unload command was applied or if you want to check if a referenced drawing has changed since you opened the master.

List View   Tree View   Click on the headings to sort the list

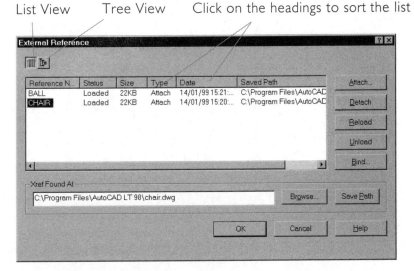

On a project that involves the use of xrefs, it should be agreed about the location of all xrefs and the layering system in use.

Save Path

Save Path save the path to the folder that contains the referenced file. If the xref is moved you can use Browse and reset the path in this way.

List View

List View simply lists the attached files. Clicking on the headings Size, Type, etc, will sort the files under the selected heading.

Tree View

Tree View provides more detailed information about the xrefs than the List View.

Xrefs and the List Command

The terms xref and external reference have the same meaning.

The list command may be used to check information about any object in a drawing. Type List at the command line and click on the xrefs in the master drawing. In the example below, the ball and chair were selected. Both are externally referenced drawings.

The List command is useful if you have to look at someone else's drawing. It can be applied to any AutoCAD LT object.

A scale factor of I means the drawing was referenced as it was drawn (ie, no scaling)

```
AutoCAD LT Text Window                                              _□×
 Edit
Select objects:
                    BLOCK REFERENCE  Layer: 0
                            Space: Model space
                    Handle = EC
                    BALL
                    External reference
                at point, X= 194.7266  Y= 254.0092  Z=   0.0000
                    X scale factor    1.0000
                    Y scale factor    1.0000
            rotation angle      0
                    Z scale factor    1.0000

                    BLOCK REFERENCE  Layer: 0
                            Space: Model space
                    Handle = F2
                    CHAIR
                    External reference
                at point, X= 204.0512  Y= 251.6924  Z=   0.0000
                    X scale factor    1.0000
                    Y scale factor    1.0000
            rotation angle      0
                    Z scale factor    1.0000

Press ENTER to continue:
```

The chair is still an xref

The list command will give information on all xrefs in a drawing if '-xref' is issued at the command line and the '?' option is used.

```
AutoCAD LT Text Window                                              _□×
 Edit
Press ENTER to continue:

Command:
LIST
Select objects: *Cancel*

Command: -xref

?/Bind/Detach/Path/Unload/Reload/Overlay/<Attach>: ?

Xref(s) to list <*>:

Xref name                      Xref Type   Path
-------------------            ---------   ----------

BALL                           Attach      C:\Program Files\AutoCAD LT
98\ball.dwg
CHAIR                          Attach      C:\Program Files\AutoCAD LT
98\chair.dwg

Total Xref(s): 2

Command: |
```

Content Explorer

The Content Explorer is AutoCAD LT's own file manager. It will help you to do the following:

- See visually the blocks and xrefs in a drawing file.

- Insert blocks and xrefs by just dragging them into the drawing.

- Copy drawings and blocks from one folder to another.

- Group files needed for the same project together.

- Search for files on the disk or network.

The Content Explorer is found under the Insert drop-down menu. When it is opened, the default display shows the blocks present in the current drawing. A list of tabs show groupings of files. A tree view of the disk or a network can be displayed and a Preview of a block or xref.

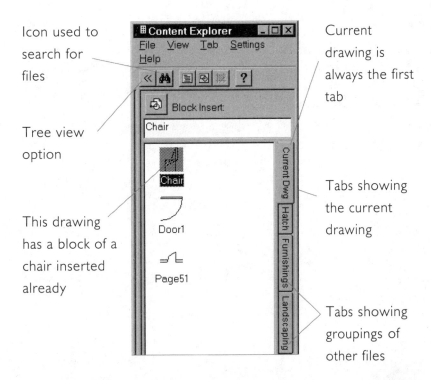

Icon used to search for files

Tree view option

This drawing has a block of a chair inserted already

Current drawing is always the first tab

Tabs showing the current drawing

Tabs showing groupings of other files

...cont'd

Inserting blocks

The Content Explorer tabs allow you to group files according to a project. AutoCAD LT has grouped the sample files under headings such as 'Landscaping', 'Kitchen' and 'House Design'. You can view these by clicking on a tab. Try the following:

1 Open an existing drawing or start up a new one. Open the Content Explorer (Insert > Content Explorer). From the File menu in the Content Explorer select 'Block Insert'.

2 Click on the Landscape tab. A list of symbols related to landscaping is displayed.

3 Drag one of the symbols, such as a tree, over to the current drawing.

AutoCAD LT 98 allows you to use the Content Explorer to place hatching in a drawing. See Chapter Thirteen.

4 Change to the 'Current.dwg' tab. The symbols you dragged across will be listed as part of the drawing. The symbol can be inserted again and again from the library.

5 To view the symbol in the library in greater detail, select the Preview icon.

Detail of the selected block

...cont'd

Creating new tab

A tab can be created for a folder or a particular drawing. Use Explorer's tree to move to the folder or file you want to use. In the example below, a folder will be created on the desktop and then a tab will be created for that folder.

 You can rename a tag by double-clicking on it.

1 Create a folder on the desktop using the normal procedure for Windows. Name the folder LT Project. You can minimize AutoCAD LT to do this.

2 Open an existing drawing or start up a new one. Open the Content Explorer (Insert > Content Explorer) and click on the icon « . This will display all the folders on your computer. Look for the LT Project folder and single-click on it to highlight it.

3 In tree view (that is at the top of your list of folders) click on the Create Tab button.

4 The current folder name is offered as the default. Keep this by clicking OK.

 A tab can be deleted by right-clicking it and selecting Delete from the menu.

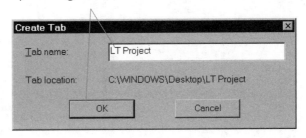

5 The tab is added to the list of tabs. If you don't like its location you can drag it to a new position.

Copying and moving drawings

Now that a tab is set up for a project you may copy/move drawing files into it. Before you can do this you must make sure that a tab points to a folder. Follow the steps below to move a file from the sample folder to the LT Project tab.

HANDY TIP

To copy a file, hold down the Ctrl key while dragging the file in step 2.

1 Click on the LT Project tab to make it current. In tree view find the sample folder. Double-click on it to view its contents.

2 Drag one of the drawings shown in the Content Explorer (not the tree) over to the tab LT Project and drop it. The file will be moved to the tab.

HANDY TIP

The Content Explorer can be used to copy and move files in a manner similar to **Windows Explorer (Windows 95 and later versions) and File Manager (Windows 3.xx).**

3 In tree view click on the Create Tab button.

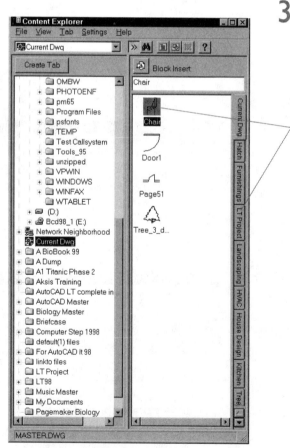

Drag this file to the LT Project tab

Note that the sample folder is open

Searching Using the Content Explorer

Click on the search icon or use the menu View > Find. To search for a file that begins with 'flo' try the following:

1 Type 'flo*' in here. The '*' symbol means any other characters. This search will find a file like 'floor.dwg'. The search will only look for AutoCAD LT drawing files.

Search results can be saved by using File > Save Results in the AutoCAD LT Find dialogue box.

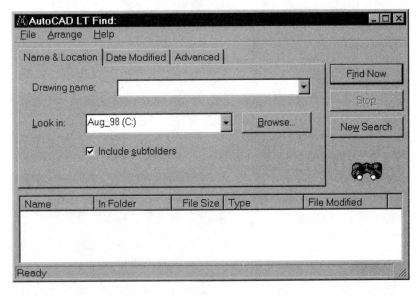

Use the Date Modified tab if you know the date the file was last worked on.

2 Click the C: drive from the options here (or what ever drive your AutoCAD LT is on). Make sure there is a tick in the Include subfolders box. This will carry out a search in all folders that are on the C: drive.

3 Click on Find Now. The Content Explorer will look for all drawing files that begin with the letters 'flo'. The files will be listed as they are found.

The Advanced tab allows a search for blocks or attributes contained in a drawing. (Blocks are covered in detail earlier in this chapter. See Chapter Twelve for more on Attributes.)

Using the Search Results

The results of a search can be used by double-clicking on the file. The Content Explorer refreshes its tree view to show the location of the file, and the file is shown in the content view. You can work with it directly from here.

Use the Advanced search to find blocks or attribute tags.

REMEMBER

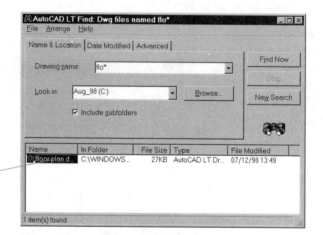

Double click on the file

The tree is updated to show its location

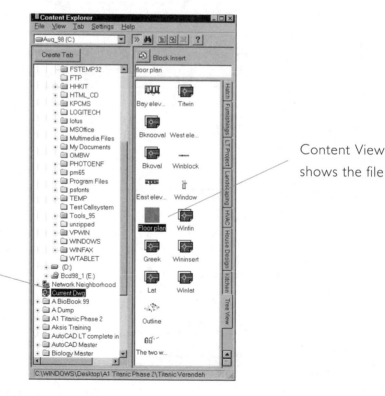

Content View shows the file

Dimensioning

The primary function of a computer aided design drawing is to supply enough information about an object to enable its construction. Dimensioning is an essential visual guide to helping someone to interpret the drawing for construction. AutoCAD LT has many tools for dimensioning drawings, positioning the dimensions and later editing them. In this chapter you will be introduced to many of these dimensioning tools and the techniques for using them.

Chapter Nine

Covers

Dimensioning

AutoCAD LT has many tools to help you to place dimensions on a drawing. There is no need to draw dimension lines or calculate a dimension value. AutoCAD LT will do this for you. Some of the terms used in conjunction with dimensioning are illustrated below.

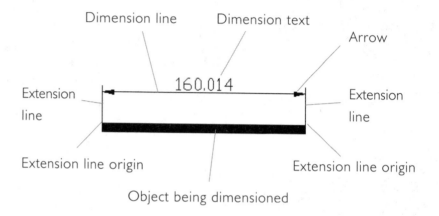

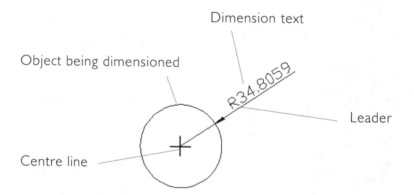

Associative dimensioning

The term associative dimensioning means that the dimension is associated with an object. When the object being dimensioned is changed, that change is shown immediately in the dimension, so there is no need to re-dimension the object. Associative dimensioning can be switched off.

The Dimensioning Toolbar

To call up the dimensioning toolbar use the View drop down menu: View > Toolbars, and place an x opposite Dimension in the list of toolbars.

Linear Dimension: dimensions horizontal and vertical lines

Aligned Dimension: dimensions lines which are not horizontal or vertical

Ordinate Dimensions: also called datum dimensions, they measure a perpendicular distance from an origin. The origin can be specified by the user

Radius Dimension: places a radius dimension on circles and arcs

Diameter Dimension: places a diameter dimension on circles

Angular Dimension: dimensions the angular distance between two objects

Baseline Dimension: allows dimensions to be measured from a datum line and stacked at a specified distance

Continue dimension: allows contiguous dimensions to be aligned

Leader Line: used for annotations

Tolerance: allows the insertion of geometric tolerances

Center Mark: places center marks on circles and arcs

Dimension Edit: allows you to reposition the dimension text

Dimension Text Edit: enables the editing of the dimension text

Dimension Style: enables the creation of styles for dimensioning in engineering or architectural drawing, etc.

Dimension Update: allows individual elements of a dimension to be updated

Linear Dimensioning

To dimension an object (it can be horizontal or vertical) follow the steps below. In this example the dimension is applied to a horizontal polyline.

1 Click on the Linear dimension icon. AutoCAD LT responds with 'First extension line origin or ENTER to select'.

2 Press the Enter key or the right mouse button and AutoCAD LT responds 'Select object to dimension'.

3 Select the polyline by picking on it. AutoCAD LT immediately calculates the length of the object and now asks 'Dimension line location?'.

Read the command line carefully throughout the dimensioning procedures.

4 To position the dimension line, move the cursor above or below the polyline and pick a point. The dimension is now locked into position.

Unhappy with how the dimension looks?

The dimension text may look too small or too big, the arrows may be the wrong size, or perhaps the extension lines run too close to the polyline. All these features can be individually modified to form a dimensioning style (see page 144). For the moment we will change all the above elements by scaling them up. The setting for the size of all the dimension elements is held in a system variable (see page 40) called DIMSCALE. By changing the dimscale value you affect the display of the dimension. Try the following:

1 Type DIMSCALE at the command line and press Enter. The response may be 'New value for DIMSCALE <1.0000>:'

2 Type in a value greater than the default value. Try 2 in this case and press Enter.

...cont'd

3 AutoCAD LT returns you to a blank line prompt. Nothing appears to have happened. You now need to update the dimension to see the effect of the new setting. Click on the Dimension Update icon .

4 Select the dimension. Selection is made by picking anywhere on the dimension (text or lines). The dimension will highlight. Press Enter.

5 All aspects of the dimension will increase in size – the arrows, the text, etc.

The dimensioned polyline when DIMSCALE was set to 1

The dimensioned polyline is shown below when the Update Dimension was applied after the DIMSCALE value was set to 3.

Dimension text increased in size

Arrows increased in size

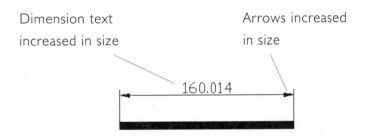

Dimscale affects the setting in the leader lines. Dimscale does not affect the actual length of a dimension or the object being dimensioned.

Object Snap and Dimensioning

The Object Snap tools may be used to tell AutoCAD LT the position of the extension lines. This is useful if you are dimensioning across several different lines. Consider the case below where a line and a polyline run end to end. The linear dimension must measure from one end of the line to the other end of the polyline.

Left ████████████████────────── Right

Polyline   Line

You can just as easily use the Object Snap toolbar instead of shift and right-click.

1 Select the Linear Dimension icon. In response to 'first extension line origin' hold the shift key down, right-click the mouse and select Endpoint from the menu.

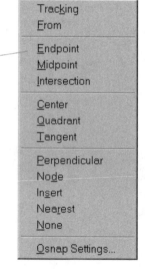

Tracking
From

Endpoint
Midpoint
Intersection

Center
Quadrant
Tangent

Perpendicular
Node
Insert
Nearest
None

Osnap Settings...

2 Move the cursor to the left end of the polyline and select. AutoCAD LT will now want to know the 'second extension line origin'. Again, hold Shift down and right-click the mouse button. Select Endpoint from the menu and pick the right end of the line.

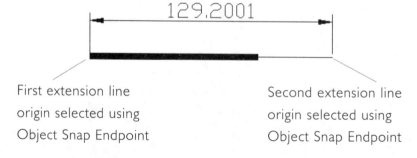

129.2001

First extension line origin selected using Object Snap Endpoint

Second extension line origin selected using Object Snap Endpoint

Ordinate Dimensioning

Introduction

Ordinate dimensions always refer back to a specific location on a drawing. In the default settings in AutoCAD LT the origin is at the bottom left of the screen. All the dimensions are based on this origin. You may setup a separate origin and mark co-ordinates on your drawing which refer to this origin. This can ensure more accuracy in a drawing, particularly for those objects drawn that might be cut by a lathe or milling machine, or which otherwise need a very high degree of accuracy.

Setting up an ordinate dimension

To switch on the Dimension toolbar click on Toolbars from the View menu.

Draw an object or two in AutoCAD LT. We will first mark an ordinate dimension, leaving the origin at the bottom left of the screen. You can switch on the icon which shows you where the origin is by following these steps:

1 Type UCS at the command line and press Enter.

2 Type On and press Enter or the spacebar.

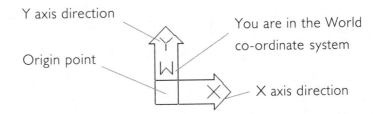

Y axis direction

Origin point

You are in the World co-ordinate system

X axis direction

Ordinate dimensions at the end of a polyline

144.232

34.778

To switch Ortho on, just double-click on the word Ortho at the bottom of the screen.

Before you proceed, it's a good idea to turn Ortho on so that the leader lines from the ordinate dimension are vertical and/or horizontal. Click on the Ordinate icon from the dimensions toolbar. Use Object Snap to select the endpoint of the entity. Click again to position the ordinate leader line along the X axis. Repeat the procedure for the Y axis.

...cont'd

In this example the origin 0,0 will be moved onto an object and an ordinate reading will then be placed at another point on the same object.

The block of the chair will be used in this illustration.

Moving the UCS

Handy Tip

Hold the Shift key down and right-click to use the Object Snap modes instead of going to the toolbar.

1 At the command line type UCS and press Enter. Respond to the prompt by typing O for origin and pressing Enter. AutoCAD LT will want to know the position of the new origin. Use Object Snap to snap to the bottom left of the chair.

Step 1 places the origin here

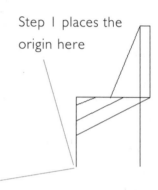

Placing the ordinate dimension

2 Click on the Ordinate icon and use Object Snap to snap to the bottom left of the chair. If you forgot to switch Ortho on, do so now. Position the X ordinate. Repeat the procedure for the Y ordinate.

The ordinate dimension 'proves' that this is the origin

3 Now place an ordinate dimension at the top right of the chair using the same procedure.

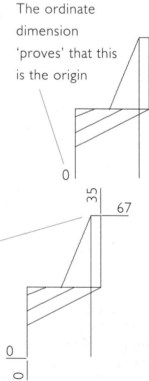

The chair with both ordinate dimensions in place

Aligned Dimensioning

The Aligned Dimension is for linear objects which are not vertical or horizontal. However, it may also be used for horizontal and vertical lines. It works the same way as the linear dimensioning on page 128.

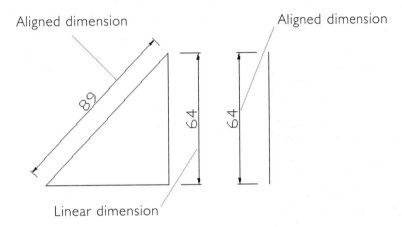

In this illustration the vertical lines were dimensioned with the Linear and Aligned options.

Center Mark

A Center Mark shows the centre of circles, arcs and fillet arcs. When you click on the center mark icon ⊡ AutoCAD LT will ask you to select the arc or circle. Once you click on the circle or arc the center mark is positioned and the command ends.

The Center Mark is composed of two lines, each of which can be erased separately.

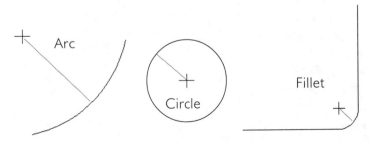

Radius and Diameter

AutoCAD LT can quickly calculate the radius and diameter of circles, arcs and fillet arcs. In the case of a radius it places the letter 'R' for radius in front of the measurement and for diameters it places the diameter symbol.

To position a radius, click on the radius icon and select the arc or circle. You can move the values into position by moving the cursor. Try placing them inside and outside a circle.

Radius

Diameter

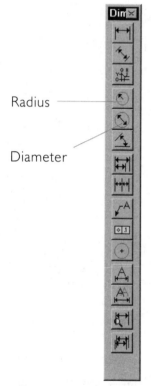

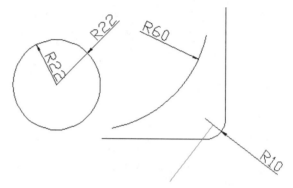

AutoCAD LT draws the dimension line from the centre of the selected arc or circle automatically.

To position a diameter, click on the Diameter icon and select the arc or circle. You can move the values into position by moving the cursor. Try placing them inside and outside a circle.

HANDY TIP

To lock the dimension-ing into vertical and horizontal positions, switch on Ortho (F8 function key) before you dimension.

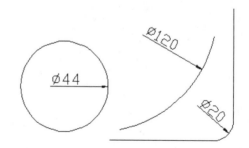

Continue Dimensioning

The Continue Dimension allows you to run a series of linear dimensions which are always positioned at the same level. You can see an example in the illustration below. The first value of 33 was put into place using the Linear Dimension option and the 45 value was input using the Continue option. AutoCAD LT automatically lined up the 45 value with the 33 value. This is what the Continue option does.

To try this, draw a shape similar to that shown below. Here are the steps involved:

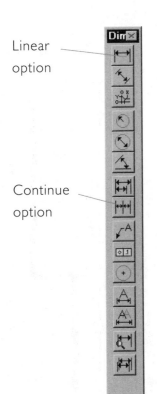

Linear option

Continue option

1 Place the 33 on the first line segment in the usual way using the Linear option (your value does not have to be 33).

2 Now select the Continue option. AutoCAD LT will ask for a 'Second extension line origin' (not a first!). Pick the end of the second line segment. The dimension line is aligned correctly. Press Enter twice to end the command.

End of second line segment

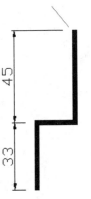

Using Continue on existing dimensions

If you try to use Continue on a dimension you did some time ago (say during a previous drawing session) AutoCAD LT will ask you to pick the dimension you want to 'continue' from by prompting 'Select continued dimension'. Pick the existing dimension and proceed as above when you see the prompt 'Second extension line origin'.

BEWARE

Position the first dimension with care as AutoCAD LT will align all the other dimensions up with it.

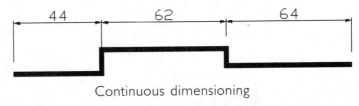

Continuous dimensioning

Baseline Dimensioning

Baseline dimensioning will refer all dimensions back to a datum line. The dimensions are stacked one above the other. The distance separating the dimensions is controlled by the system variable DIMDLI. You may also control it using the Geometry option of the Dimensioning styles (see page 146).

To try this dimensioning, draw a line like the one below. Here are the steps involved:

A datum line is a reference point.

1   Place the 175.5 dimension value on the first segment using the Linear Dimension option (your value does not have to be 175.5).

2   Click on the Baseline icon and respond to the prompt 'Specify a second extension line origin' by using Object Snap to pick at point B in the illustration.

3   The dimension line is positioned a preset distance (which can be changed) out from the first dimension line.

4   AutoCAD LT again asks for 'a second extension line origin'. Pick point C and press Enter twice to finish the command.

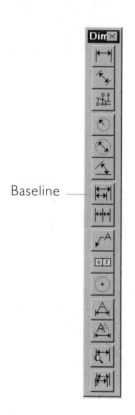

Baseline

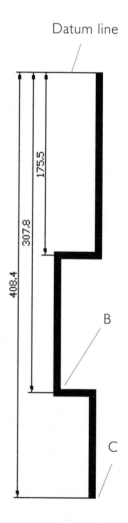

Angular Dimensioning

HANDY TIP

As you move the cursor to position the dimension line, notice how AutoCAD LT will place the arrows outside the angle as you move toward the apex of the angle.

Acute and obtuse angles can be measured using the Angular Dimensioning option. Draw some lines in the shape of 'z' to practice applying angular dimensions.

1 Click on the Angular icon.

2 In response to 'select arc, circle or line', click on a line.

3 To the second response 'Second line', select the second line. As you move the cursor you will see AutoCAD LT offering you various dimensioning formats. Try moving the cursor along the area within the acute angle and click when you like the format.

Try the same for the obtuse angle. All the angles below were placed by moving the cursor into different positions.

Angular ————

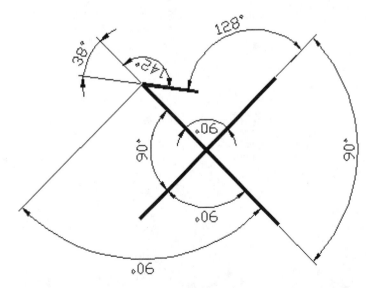

When the Angular Dimension option is selected, the prompt asks 'Select arc, circle, line, or press to ENTER:'. The effect of choosing the circle is illustrated below: just pick two points on the circle to measure the angle between them. Similarly, the sweep of an arc can be measured thus:

The term arrow in dimension-ing is used to describe any symbol at the end of a dimension or leader line. That includes ticks and dots.

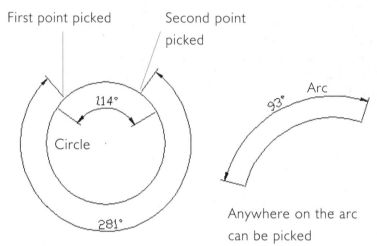

First point picked

Second point picked

Circle

Arc

Anywhere on the arc can be picked

Leader Lines

Leader lines are used to add annotations to drawings. Leader lines can be created with or without arrows; they may also have straight lines or splines. A leader has a flat section for text called a 'landing' or 'dogleg'.

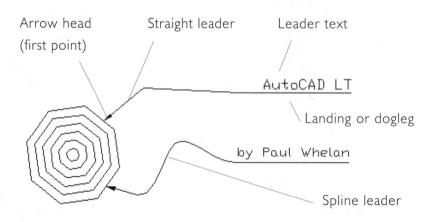

Arrow head (first point)

Straight leader

Leader text

AutoCAD LT

Landing or dogleg

by Paul Whelan

Spline leader

...cont'd

To place a leader line in a drawing, follow the steps below:

1 Select the Leader icon.
AutoCAD LT asks 'From point:'.
Pick a point in the usual way
(Object Snap is available).

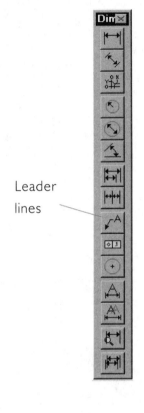

2 By default you will be given an
arrowhead and are then asked
to pick the second point. Do so.
This defines the leader line.

Leader
lines

3 The default option now is to
enter the <Annotation>. To
accept the default, press Enter,
type 'a' and press Enter again.
The mtext (multiline text)
prompt is displayed. Type in the
text you want and press Enter
twice to finish the command.

BEWARE

**The leader
arrows and
text size
can be set
in a dimension
style.**

Some of the other options
Format: This option is chosen by typing 'f' for format.
Under it you will find the options to use a 'Spline' or
change back to a 'Straight Leader Line'. The arrow can be
removed by selecting 'None'. You may exit the format
options list by typing 'e' for exit.

Annotation: By pressing Enter twice when this default is
offered you will see the options for 'Tolerances', 'Copy',
'Block', 'None' and 'mtext'.

Editing a Dimension

The text that is part of a dimension cannot be edited with the normal text commands 'mtext' and 'dtext'. There are several ways to edit the dimension text:

Command line: 'dimtedit'

Menu: Dimensions > Align Text

Use grips

Dimensions > Align Text

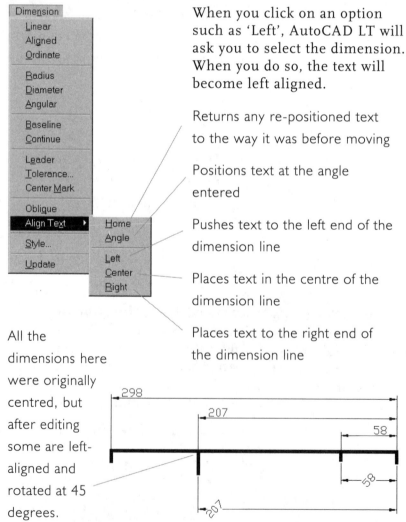

When you click on an option such as 'Left', AutoCAD LT will ask you to select the dimension. When you do so, the text will become left aligned.

Returns any re-positioned text to the way it was before moving

Positions text at the angle entered

Pushes text to the left end of the dimension line

Places text in the centre of the dimension line

Places text to the right end of the dimension line

All the dimensions here were originally centred, but after editing some are left-aligned and rotated at 45 degrees.

If you are constantly editing dimensions, you should consider setting up a dimensioning style.

You can select several dimensions at once and apply the edit changes to all the dimensions.

Typing 'dimtedit' at the command line offers the same options of Left, Right, Center, Home and Angle. However, it also allows you to reposition the text using the cursor. Try executing the command now. AutoCAD LT will ask you to select the text for editing. The moment the dimension is selected the dimension text will move with the cursor. Simply pick a new location to reposition it. The extension lines will also follow the cursor movement so that you can lengthen or shorten them.

This dimension had the text moved to a new position and the extension lines stretched. See the original dimension on the previous page.

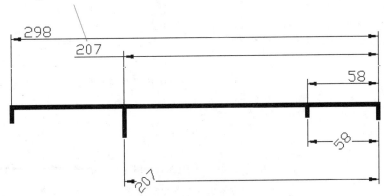

Using Grips to edit a dimension

Click on the dimension when the command line is blank. The grips will appear. Notice the grip at the centre point of the text. This grip can be selected by clicking on it. The text can then be moved into position.

This grip can be used to move the text or stretch the extension lines

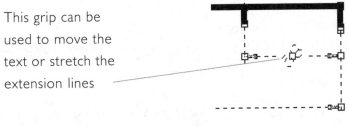

The DIMEDIT Command

Dimedit allows you to easily replace the dimension text itself. The command is typed at the command line. Each of the options is described here.

Home: Returns the text to the position it had before it was moved.

Rotate: Rotates the dimension text.

Oblique: Repositions the extension lines at a new angle. The default position is at 90 degrees to the dimension line. An obliquing angle of 45 degrees is shown in the illustration below.

The extension lines may be controlled by setting up a dimension style.

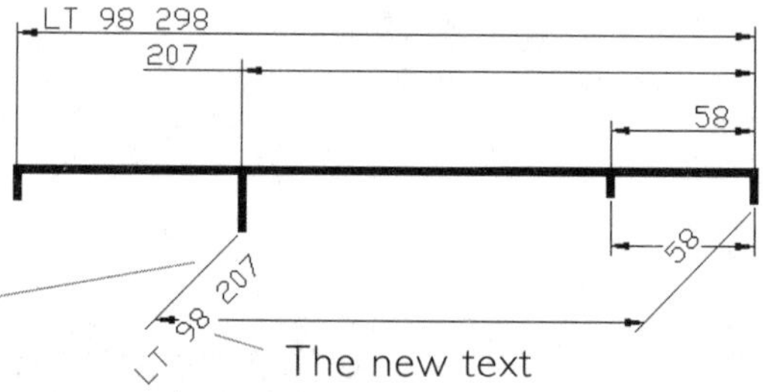

New: Allows you to replace the dimension text. Once the option New is selected, the Multiline Text Editor is open. Just type the new text in the editor and click OK. The old text is represented by <>. To remove the old text you must remove these symbols in the Multiline Text Editor.

The extension lines were set to an angle of 45 degrees using the oblique option

The new text

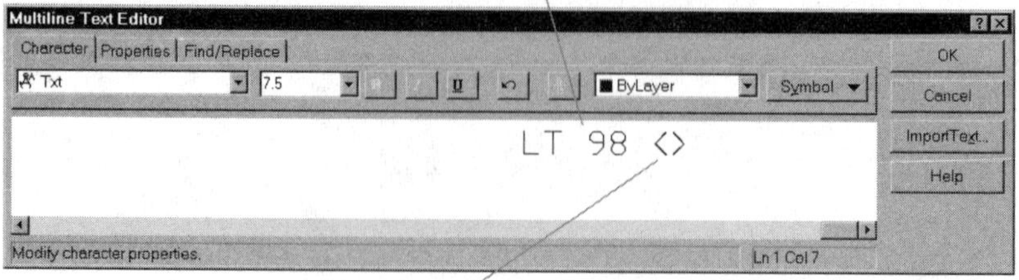

The markers '< >' symbolise the old text. If you leave these here the old text will remain

Dimension Styles and Tolerances

The various settings which control how a dimension appears can be stored as a dimension style. Several different styles may be created and used when needed. This chapter shows you how to create these styles.

Covers

Chapter Ten

Dimension Styles

All the elements that make up a dimension can be modified to form a dimension style. For example, you might have oblique extension lines with the dimension text always above the line. These settings can be saved with a name and later applied when dimensioning objects. Styles give a drawing or a project visual consistency.

Menu: Dimensions>Style...

The Dimension Styles dialogue box is used to define a style.

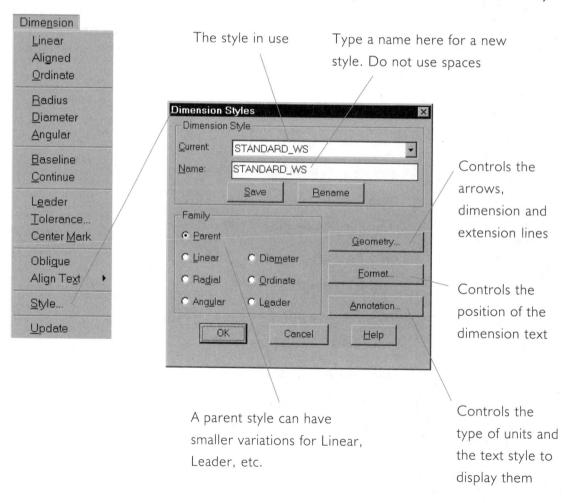

The style in use

Type a name here for a new style. Do not use spaces

Controls the arrows, dimension and extension lines

Controls the position of the dimension text

A parent style can have smaller variations for Linear, Leader, etc.

Controls the type of units and the text style to display them

How to Create a Style

The following steps will illustrate how a basic style is created. This style will be used to dimension the exterior of a building as shown on an architectural drawing. Its basic features are to use a tick instead of an arrow and to place the dimension text on the left extension line, as shown in the illustration.

Text aligned vertically on the left

114

Tick

HANDY TIP

A new style can be created from an existing style. This allows you to build up a library of styles without having to define all the elements each time.

1 From the drop-down menu click on Dimension>Style...

2 Highlight the existing name and type in 'Exterior'.

3 Click on the Geometry button. In the section marked Arrowheads click on the down arrow to the right of '1st'. From the list select 'Architectural Tick'. In the 'Size' box type in 4. Click on OK.

4 Click on the Format button. In the Horizontal Justification box click a few times on the actual image of the dimension. See how the various justification positions are illustrated. Stop clicking when the justification is similar to that in the illustration above.

5 Click OK. You are now back at the Dimension Styles dialogue box again. Click Save to save the changes and then click OK to leave the dialogue box.

6 A dimension style has been created. Draw a line and place a linear dimension on it. It should look like the one at the top of this page.

If you create several different styles, make sure that the one you want to use is current.

Some Geometry Settings

The geometry settings control the appearance of the dimension lines, the extension lines, the arrow heads and the centre marks.

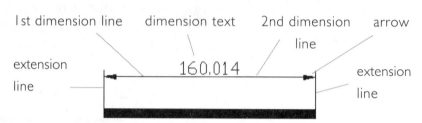

1st dimension line   dimension text   2nd dimension line   arrow

extension line

160.014

extension line

'Suppressing the 1st' tells AutoCAD LT not to draw the first half of the dimension line

Refers to the baseline offsets

Click to select different 'arrows'

Setting a colour allows you to specify a pen thickness at plot time

The 1st extension line is the first point you selected when dimensioning the object

Sets the length of the extension line above the dimension line

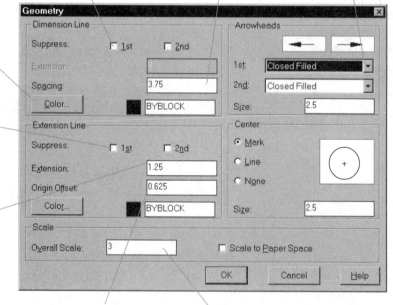

Sets the gap between the object being dimensioned and the start of the extension line

This sets the overall size for the dimension text, the arrow size and extension lines. It is the same as the system variable DIMSCALE

Geometry Examples

Here are some styles based on modifications to the Geometry options in the Dimension Styles dialogue box.

Any of these features can be saved as a new dimension style.

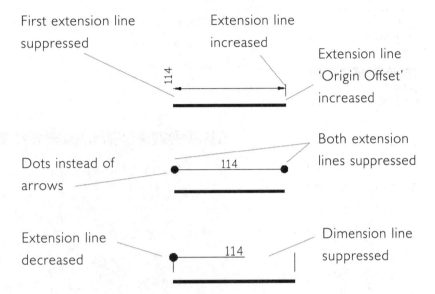

First extension line suppressed

Extension line increased

Extension line 'Origin Offset' increased

Dots instead of arrows

Both extension lines suppressed

Extension line decreased

Dimension line suppressed

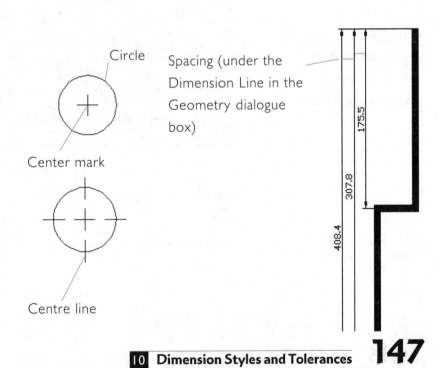

Circle

Center mark

Centre line

Spacing (under the Dimension Line in the Geometry dialogue box)

Some Format Settings

The Format dialogue box allows you to control where the text will appear on the dimension.

Insert/remove a tick to control the inside and outside settings independently

Click several times here to see the various ways the text can be positioned

Sometimes the dimension text and arrows are too big to fit between the extension lines. This option allows you to force specific settings such as 'arrows only'

Allows the text to be centered between the extension lines or actually beside them...

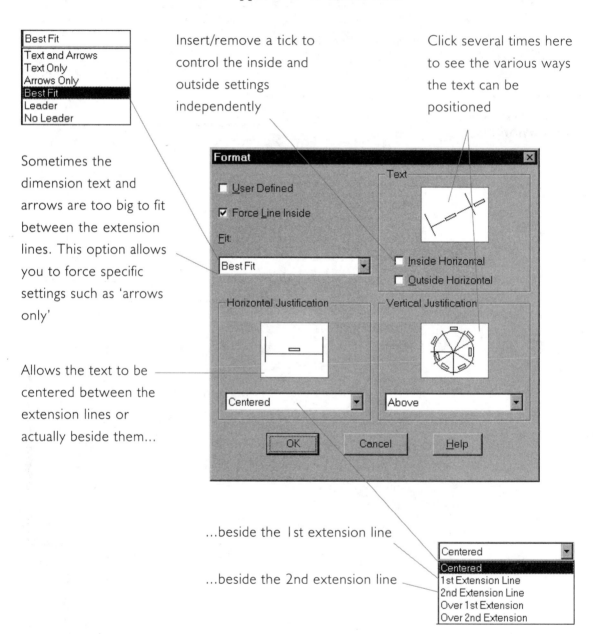

...beside the 1st extension line

...beside the 2nd extension line

Format Examples

These examples show the affect of the Fit option with regard to fitting the arrows and text inside the extension lines. AutoCAD LT will try to carry out what you have set if it is possible, otherwise it will make the decision itself as to what looks the best.

You can still use the Edit Dimension option to move the text to a new position.

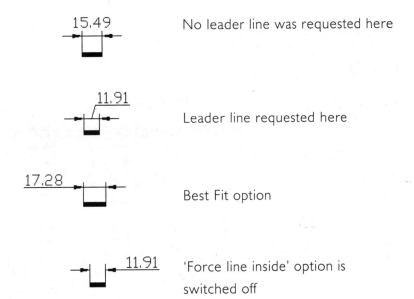

No leader line was requested here

Leader line requested here

Best Fit option

'Force line inside' option is switched off

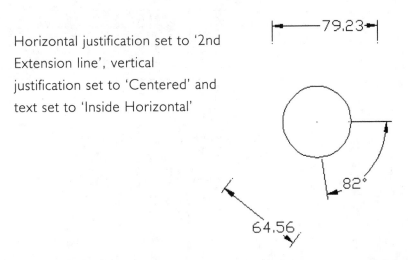

Horizontal justification set to '2nd Extension line', vertical justification set to 'Centered' and text set to 'Inside Horizontal'

Some Annotation Settings

The Annotation settings affect how the dimension text appears.

Allows you to display two different unit systems

Sets the number of decimal places displayed in a dimension

If you have already defined text styles, they can be used here

Allows a prefix or suffix such as mm to accompany the dimension text

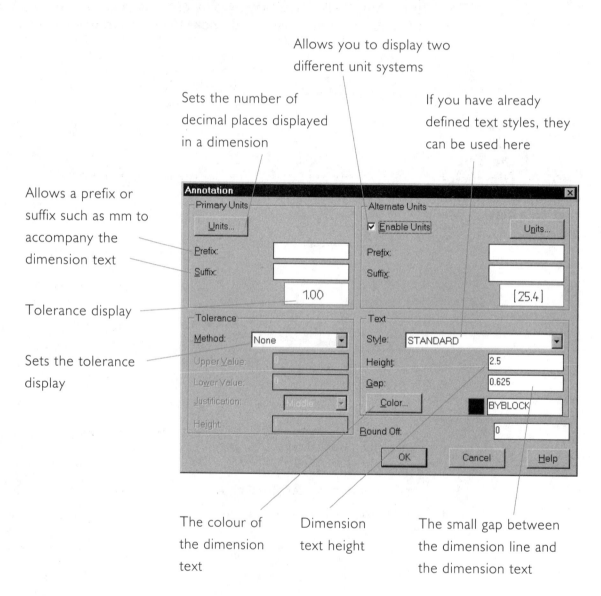

Tolerance display

Sets the tolerance display

The colour of the dimension text

Dimension text height

The small gap between the dimension line and the dimension text

Annotation Examples

Increased text height   Precision is 0.0

Increased gap

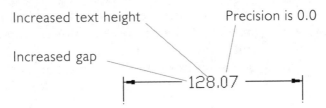

|— 128.07 —|

When a style is updated, any existing dimensions in that style are also updated.

Alternate units enabled
– feet & inches

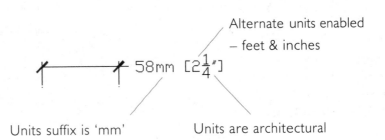

58mm [2¼"]

Units suffix is 'mm'   Units are architectural

Suffix is set to 'all lengths'   Precision 0.00

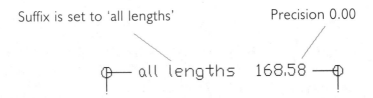

all lengths   168.58

Units suffix is 'mm'

122°mm

Ø51mm

Two different 'arrows'
are used

Styles Using Tolerances

Tolerances can be added to a dimension style. A tolerance can show the range of error or acceptability in the manufacture of a product. The tolerance settings are found in Annotation settings of the Dimension Styles dialogue box. The Tolerance options used by AutoCAD LT are as follows:

The number of decimal places shown in the dimension text and the tolerance can be set independently.

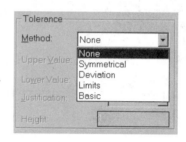

Symmetrical:	the values are given the same upper and lower limit
Deviation:	a variation that has a different plus and minus value
Limits:	actually adds/subtracts values you specify to the dimension text value
Basic:	places a box around the basic dimension text value

A suffix or prefix attached to a dimension will also show on a tolerance. This may make the dimensioning text a bit too long!

The number of decimal points shown in the tolerances is controlled by the Primary Units button 'Units'.

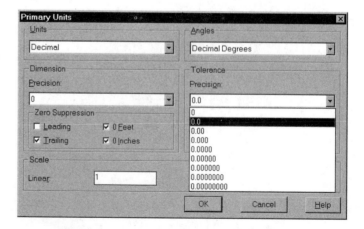

Examples of Tolerances

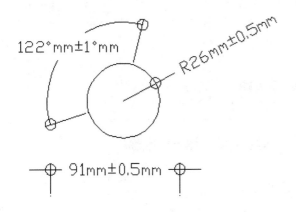

122°mm±1°mm R26mm±0.5mm

91mm±0.5mm

122°mm +1°mm / 0°mm   R26mm +1.0mm / 0.0mm

91mm +1.0mm / 0.0mm

Symmetrical: the values are given the same upper and lower limit of 0.5

Deviation: a variation that has a different plus and minus value. The plus value is 1 and the minus value is 0

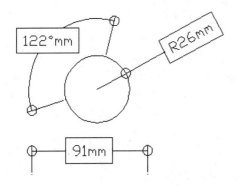

122°mm R26mm

91mm

122°mm / 121°mm   R26.2mm / 25.0mm

91.7mm / 90.5mm

Basic: places a box around the basic dimension text value

Limits: actually adds/subtracts values you specify to the dimension text value, in this case 0.8 is added and 0.4 is subtracted from the correctly measured dimension value

Building up Dimension Styles

In this case three dimensioning styles have been created: one for the exterior of a building, another for the interior and the third for adding annotations.

HANDY TIP

If you set up a template file, define all your styles within it so that they are available in all your drawings.

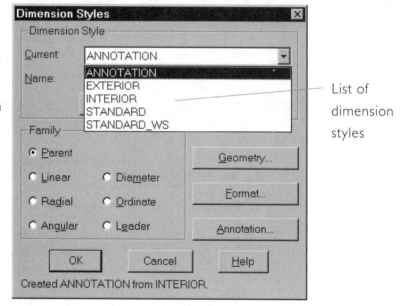

List of dimension styles

Any style can be used as the basis for the next style so be careful of the style you have in the 'Current' box before you make modifications to define the new style.

Families

Once a style is created, small variations within it can be saved without having to create a new style. For example, if you create a style for dimensioning the exterior of a building, then you may like to create a style within it that can be used for ordinate dimensions.

Once the Exterior style has been created, make sure it is listed as 'current', and then click on Ordinate and proceed to make modifications relating to Ordinate dimensioning.

Attribute Creation

In this chapter, you'll learn how to attribute text to the graphical images. This text can hold information about the drawing and may later be separated from the drawing objects and placed into a word processor, spreadsheet or database application as a bill of materials.

Covers

Chapter Eleven

What is an Attribute?

The creation and insertion of blocks into a drawing speeds up the drawing process considerably and adds consistency to drawings. Frequently it is necessary to insert text beside a block to indicate its characteristics. For example, when drawing an electric circuit, the symbol for a battery may be inserted as a block and later the voltage may need to be added in as text beside it.

Instead of writing the voltage in as text beside the block (using dtext for example) each time it is inserted, AutoCAD LT allows you to attribute the text to the block. This implies that each time the block is inserted the text is also inserted.

An attribute is text attached to a block.

Using attributes can be even more sophisticated than that. An attribute may be defined so that AutoCAD LT will ask you for the voltage each time the block is inserted. At a later stage the voltage value can be extracted from the drawing and used in another program such as a word processor, database or spreadsheet. It is this ability to extract information from a block that makes the concept of attributes so valuable.

More than one attribute can be attached to a block.

Attributes can be defined as textual data attached to a block. In the example below a block of a wheel has four different attributes attached to it. When the wheel was inserted into the drawing, AutoCAD LT asked 'How many spokes?', 'Lightweight or Heavyweight?', 'Diameter of the wheel?' and 'The Cost?'. These questions were originally programmed in by you, the user. You will learn how to do this in the following pages.

12
Lightweight
22
56

Each one is a user defined attribute attached to the wheel

Block of a wheel

Creating your First Attribute

AutoCAD LT will ask you for some information when you are defining an attribute. The most important of these are explained below.

A tag: an everyday example of a tag can be seen by looking at any official form you might fill in for, say, tax purposes. The box where you type in your name will be preceded by the word 'Name:'. This 'Name:' is a tag in AutoCAD LT language.

A prompt: this is the question or comment you want to appear when the block is being inserted. For example, 'What is your name?'

A value: this is the default value and would be the most common value you may use. For example, with respect to the bicycle wheels, the company might manufacture more 28" wheels than any other size, so 28" would be a sensible default value.

The mode: this really concerns the visibility of the attribute value on the screen. You can define an attribute as being invisible. If you do so then you must switch the attribute visibility on if you wish to see it at a later stage. An attribute can also be defined as constant. In this case AutoCAD LT will not ask you for a value when you are inserting the block.

You should be familiar with blocks before you work with attributes.

If you want to use a text style other than the STANDARD, you should define it before trying to create attributes.

The other steps in defining the attribute are similar to block creation and text insertion.

The insertion point refers to the point at which the block will be attached to the cross hairs when it is being placed in the drawing. Use object snap to select it accurately.

The text options are the usual ones of justification, text height and rotation. If you want to use a text style you must have defined it first.

The following pages describe attribute creation in detail.

Steps to Attribute Creation

1   To complete the exercise over the next few pages you should draw a simplified wheel, as on the previous page before you start defining the attributes.

2   From the Draw drop-down menu click on Block and then Define Attribute…

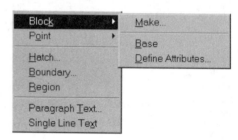

3   The Attribute Definition dialogue box appears with the cursor flashing in the Tag edit box. Type in the tag 'spoke_no'. Do not use spaces.

4   Next type in the prompt you want to appear on the screen when you are inserting the block of the wheel. Try 'How many spokes?'

Type in the tag here   This will appear when the block is being inserted   Default number of spokes

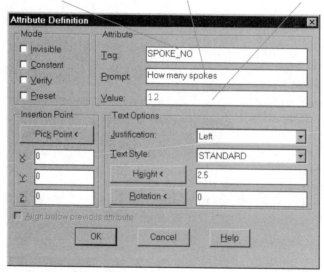

...cont'd

You can proceed to the next page after step 8 if you just want to see the single attribute in action.

5 Imagine that more 12 spoke wheels are made than any other. 12 would then be a wise default value. AutoCAD LT will offer this value when you insert the block. You can of course override it. Type in 12 in the Value edit box.

6 Now you select the position for the tag beside the wheel. In the Insertion point section of the dialogue box click on 'Pick Point <'. You will be returned to the drawing. Pick a point to the right and just above the wheel (around the 2 o'clock position). You will be returned to the dialogue box.

An attribute can be defined as invisible by picking Invisible in the Mode section of the dialogue box.

7 In the Text Options section select 'Height' and show AutoCAD LT the height of the text by picking a point just above the insertion point.

8 Leave the rotation angle at 0 (horizontal) and click on OK. You have finished defining the first attribute for the number of spokes. Your screen should now look like this:

SPOKE_NO————The defined attribute: the tag is left visible until you block it later

Proceed with defining the other attributes. Give them the following specifications, and then click on 'Invisible' in Mode after each specification:

Tag – WEIGHT;   Value – Lightweight

Tag – DIAMETER;   Value – 22

Tag – PRICE;   Value – 56

Lastly, to block the wheel and attributes see the next page.

Creating a Block with Attributes

When you have defined the four attributes, your AutoCAD LT screen will look like this:

You will now need to block the wheel and the attributes.

You can redefine blocks and attach attributes to them.

| From the Draw drop-down menu click on Block and then Make...

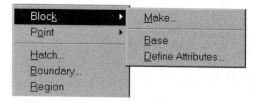

2 Enter the name 'wheel' and click on Select objects.

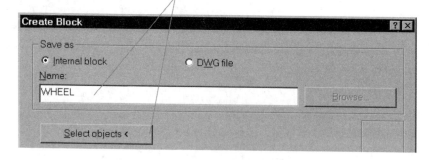

AutoCAD LT will warn you that a block exists if you try to redefine it.

3 A selection box is pulled around both the wheel and the attributes. Click on Apply and then Close.

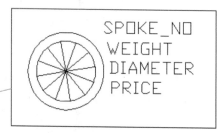

Inserting a Block with Attributes

In order to ensure that your computer and this text book are using the same settings, set the system variable ATTDIA to 1 (use the command line).

1   From the Insert menu click on Block...

HANDY TIP

A block can be inserted by typing 'insert' at the command line.

2   Select the block 'wheel' and click OK. You will be asked for the scaling on the X and Y axis and the rotation angle. Press Enter to accept the defaults.

3   The Enter Attributes dialogue box is displayed, showing the default values you entered when defining the attributes. You can accept these by clicking on OK or edit each of the values.

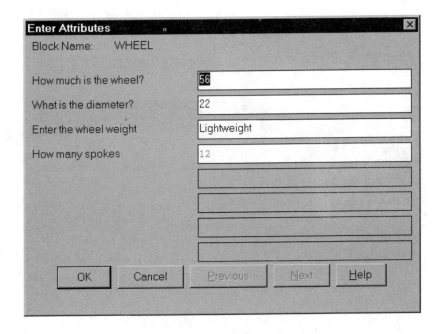

4   The block will be displayed with the attributes beside it. Notice that the value Lightweight did not appear because it was defined as being invisible. It can be made visible.

Visibility of Attributes

Attributes may end up cluttering a drawing. However, their visibility can be controlled. There are three options:

If you have been given a drawing created by someone else, try checking the visibility of attributes. They may have just been switched off.

1 'Normal' mode refers to the way the attribute was defined. If 'Invisible' was ticked in the Mode option in the Attribute Definition dialogue box, then in normal mode this is invisible.

2 'On' makes all the attributes visible, regardless of how they were defined.

3 'Off' makes all the attributes invisible, regardless of how they were defined.

The visibility of the attributes is controlled from the View drop-down menu. Click on View > Display > Attribute Display.

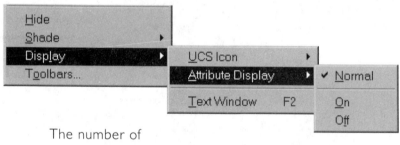

You cannot control the visibility of individual attributes: they are either all on, off or normal.

The number of spokes is visible. All the other attributes are invisible

All the attributes are made visible

Normal mode

On mode

Attribute Editing and Extraction

In this chapter, the procedure for editing attribute values in a drawing is explained. Also, the important step of extracting data from a drawing is treated in detail. This is the procedure for creating a Bill of Materials.

Chapter Twelve

Covers

Attribute Editing

After a block with attributes has been inserted, you may need to change the values in the attribute. You can do this to the attributes individually or globally. To edit attribute values individually, follow the steps below:

1 From the Modify menu select Object > Attribute > Single...

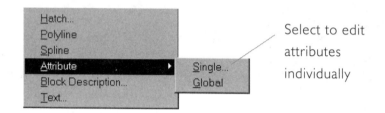

Select to edit attributes individually

HANDY TIP

Attributes do not have to be visible beside the block in order to edit them.

2 The command line prompts you to select the block which has the attributes. Select a block. The Edit Attributes dialogue box appears.

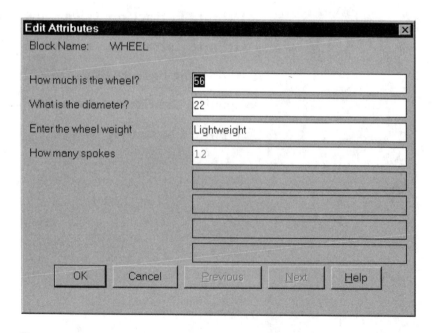

3 Click on the attribute value you want to change and modify it. Click OK when you are finished.

...cont'd

Attributes can be edited globally. This means that all values in a particular tag can be changed from the existing values to new ones. Suppose you want to change all the values 'Lightweight' to 'Featherweight'. Carry out the following steps:

1 From the Modify menu select Object > Attribute > Global.

2 Read the command line carefully during this operation. The prompt is 'Edit attributes one at a time? <Y>'. Type N for no and press Enter.

3 The prompt now reads 'Edit only attributes visible on the screen? <Y>'. Type N for no and press Enter.

HANDY TIP

If you have forgotten the name of the tag, just explode the block and the tag names will be displayed. Write them down and then undo the Explode command.

4 AutoCAD LT now wants to know the 'Block name specification'. In other words, type in the name of the block, 'wheel' in this case, and press Enter.

5 Now type in the tag name you are interested in modifying globally. In this case it is 'weight'. Press Enter.

6 Next, enter the value you want to change – in this case it is 'Lightweight' – and press Enter.

7 AutoCAD LT will tell you how many attributes it found and then ask you 'String to change'. A string is a group of letters. Type in 'Light' and press Enter.

8 You will now see the prompt 'New String'. Type in Heavy. AutoCAD LT will convert Lightweight to Heavyweight.

Attribute Extraction – Overview

When a drawing is finished it may be desirable to separate all the values attached to blocks and use them in a word processor, or some other application such as a database or spreadsheet. This, in effect, is the method for creating a bill of materials. For example, if a drawing contained seventy or eighty wheels with the attributes defined in the last chapter, you may like to find out what the total cost of all the wheels is. To do that you must separate the values out from the drawing of the wheel. This is called attribute extraction. Over the next few pages we will look at how to do this. An overview of the steps involved is outlined here.

HANDY TIP

AutoCAD LT can also tell you the number of blocks in the drawing when you are extracting values from any tag.

1 You must write a special file to tell AutoCAD LT what tags you want the values to be extracted from. This is called an extract file. Write the extract file in Notepad and give it the extension 'txt'.

2 Next, tell AutoCAD LT what blocks you want these values extracted from.

3 Data can be taken out in different ways. You will need to tell AutoCAD LT the format the data should be in for you.

4 Now supply AutoCAD LT with the name of the file you want it to put the values it has extracted into. This file is called the extract file.

5 Lastly, look at the extract file AutoCAD LT has created for you. If it is error free you may place the data into another application.

Attribute Extraction – the Detail

Let us assume that you have ten wheels in the drawing and that you want to extract the values in the PRICE tag, then place them in a spreadsheet to total all the prices.

If you have forgotten what the tags are, just explode a block. Use Undo to return it back to a block.

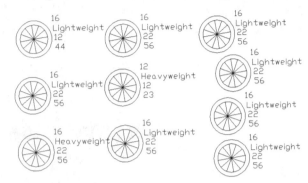

1 Start the Notepad text editor. This is usually under Accessories in Windows. Be very careful typing into the editor, especially when you reach the end of a line – never put in a space at the end of a line!

2 Type what is shown in the illustration below. Use upper-case letters for consistency.

3 Save the file with the name price.txt into a folder where you can find it later. If you are unsure about where to put it try the root of c (C:\). Note that you must give the file the extension 'txt'.

Never put in a space at the end of a line in Notepad.

A detailed explanation of the codes in this template file are on page 172.

This gives you the block name

This gives the number of blocks

This is the tag you defined

This number is explained on the next page

These are zeros

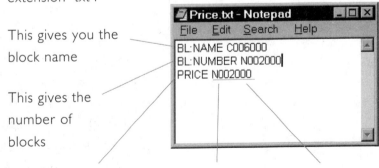

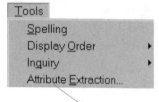

4 The template file you wrote in Notepad will be used in step 6. To start the extraction process click on the Tools drop-down menu and then Attribute Extraction. The Attribute Extraction dialogue box is displayed.

5 CDF means that each value will have commas around it. Use this option.

Leave this here. It is the extract file AutoCAD LT will make for you. It will hold the values. Its name will be the same as the drawing name, with the extension txt.

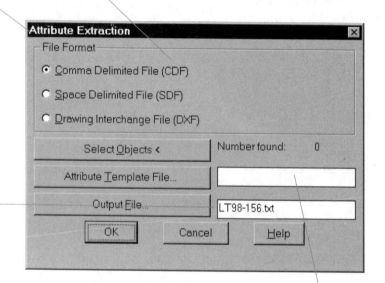

6 Click on Attribute Template File and find the file PRICE.TXT that you wrote in Notepad.

7 Click on Select Objects <. AutoCAD LT will prompt Select objects at the command line. Type ALL and press Enter (or pull a window around all the blocks).

8 If you are successful, AutoCAD LT will tell you that you have 10 records in the extract file at the command line. If you have an error, look at the template file you wrote in Notepad. It may be flawed.

Viewing the Extract File

Looking at the extract file

To check if the extract file contains the values you want, you must open it. It has the extension txt, which means that you can open it in Notepad. Here is the one you should find after carrying out the eight steps.

The first column contains the name of the block.

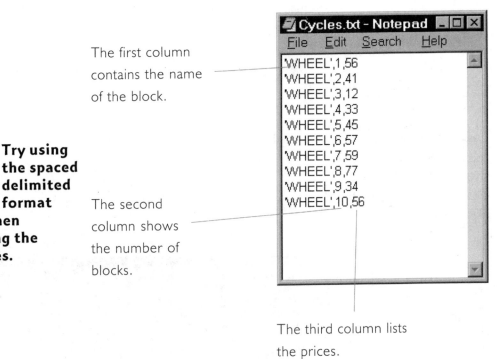

HANDY TIP

Try using the spaced delimited format (SDF) when extracting the attributes.

The second column shows the number of blocks.

The third column lists the prices.

Each column of data is separated by a comma. This is the result of the comma delimited format (CDF) you selected at the time of extraction.

Importing the Extract File into Excel

Using the extract file in Excel

This file can be inserted into another program. As an example, we will place it into the spreadsheet program MS Excel (which is a part of the Microsoft Office suite) as follows:

1 Start the Excel program. With a blank sheet on the screen, click on File > Open.

2 In the Open dialogue box select Text Files from the options under 'Files of type:'.

HANDY TIP

If you are familiar with Copy & Paste, try using it to place the extract file into Excel, or some other program.

3 Now look for the extract file, 'cycles.txt' in this case.

4 Excel will open the Text Import Wizard to try and help you make the right choices.

Place the dot in the delimited button

Sample of the file and how it will look

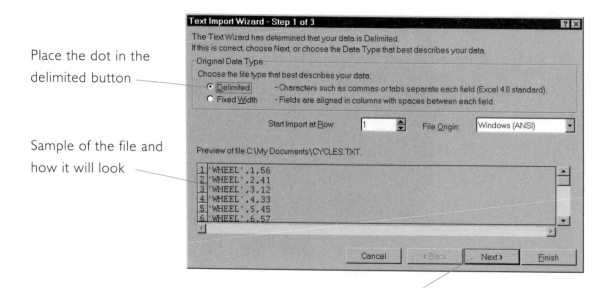

Text Import Wizard - Step 1 of 3

The Text Wizard has determined that your data is Delimited.
If this is correct, choose Next, or choose the Data Type that best describes your data.

Original Data Type

Choose the file type that best describes your data:
- Delimited - Characters such as commas or tabs separate each field (Excel 4.0 standard).
- Fixed Width - Fields are aligned in columns with spaces between each field.

Start Import at Row: 1   File Origin: Windows (ANSI)

Preview of file C:\My Documents\CYCLES.TXT.

```
1 'WHEEL',1,56
2 'WHEEL',2,41
3 'WHEEL',3,12
4 'WHEEL',4,33
5 'WHEEL',5,45
6 'WHEEL',6,57
```

Cancel   < Back   Next >   Finish

Click on Next to continue

5 Click on Next to proceed. Step 2 of 3 will appear. Place a tick in the 'Comma' box and remove the tick from any other box.

6 Click on Next. Step 3 of 3 will appear. Place a dot in the 'General' button and select Finish.

At this point the data in the extract file should fall into three columns in the Excel spreadsheet as shown below. The spreadsheet has been formatted a little, with column titles and a total calculated.

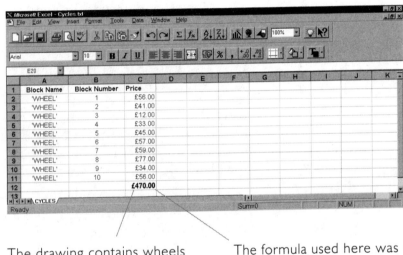

The drawing contains wheels valued at £470

The formula used here was '=sum(C2:C11)'

Template File Codes

Template file contents

Line 1	BL:NAME C006000
Line 2	BL:NUMBER N002000
Line 3	PRICE N002000

Line 1

BL:NAME tells AutoCAD LT to put the block name in the extract file. The C006000 code is made up of three parts:

1   The first part is the letter 'C'. This means that the data to be extracted is in the form of alphanumeric characters.

2   The second part of the code consists of the next three digits, '006'. These tell AutoCAD LT that the name of the block is not longer than 6 characters.

3   The third part of the code is '000'. This tells AutoCAD LT that there are no decimal places involved.

Line 2

BL:NUMBER tells AutoCAD LT to put the number of blocks in the drawing into the extract file. The N002000 code is made up of three parts:

1   The first part is the letter 'N'. This means that the data to be extracted is in the form of numbers only. These number can be used in mathematical operations later on if you like.

2   The second part of the code consists of the next three digits, '002'. These tell AutoCAD LT that the number of the block is not longer than 2 characters.

3   The third part of the code is '000'. This tells AutoCAD LT that there are no decimal places involved.

Line 3

PRICE is the tag you defined. You could include other tags in the file if you wanted to extract their values. Because PRICE is a number upon which you might later make a calculation (eg, you might total these values) you start the code with 'N'.

Chapter Thirteen

Hatching, Plotting and Viewports

AutoCAD LT has a command for applying hatch patterns to a drawing. Hatching is associative: it is associated with the objects that form its boundary. You will also learn to define your own text styles, to set up different views of a drawing and finally to print out the finished drawing.

Covers

Hatching

How the command works

The hatch command allows you to fill an area with either a solid fill or a hatch pattern. AutoCAD LT has a library of predefined hatch patterns which symbolise materials such as steel, clay, brass or concrete. You may also define simple patterns yourself (user-defined) or create a custom design from scratch using simple trigonometry. This latter custom design is beyond the scope of this text. Lastly, a solid area of colour can be applied to an enclosed area. This colour is defined by the colour of the layer the hatching is on.

Command line: bhatch

Menu: Draw>Hatch

Toolbar:

Always place hatching on a separate layer.

The command in action

On issuing the command you will need to select or define a hatch pattern. Following this you select the area you want to fill with the pattern. Lastly, you may test the pattern to see if it is okay and then apply it if you are happy with its appearance. Some hatch patterns are shown here:

A drawing with a lot of hatching can take a considerable amount of time to regenerate.

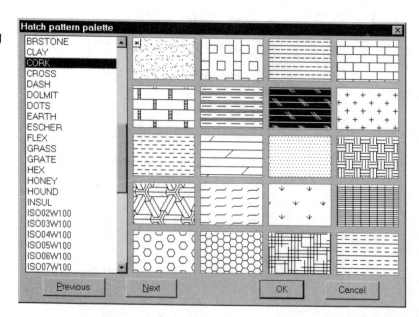

Applying a Hatch Pattern

To follow these steps, setup a drawing page of 420mm by 297mm and draw a shape similar to that shown below.

You will apply a

hatch here

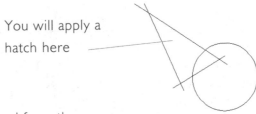

| Issue the command from the drop-down menu or type BHATCH at the command line. The Boundary Hatch dialogue box appears.

2 Click here and select the option Predefined.

3 Select Pattern...

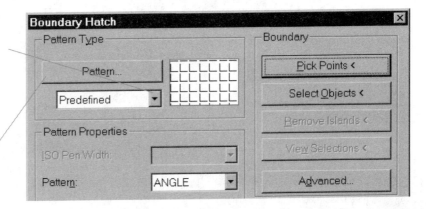

4 Click on the pattern AR-HBONE from the library.

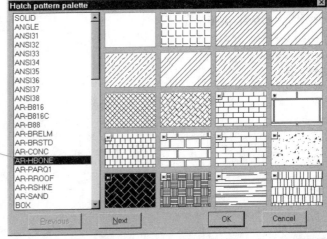

...cont'd

If you select too big a scale, the pattern may not show when it is applied.

5 Type 1.0 here.

6 To define the area to hatch, select Pick Points <.

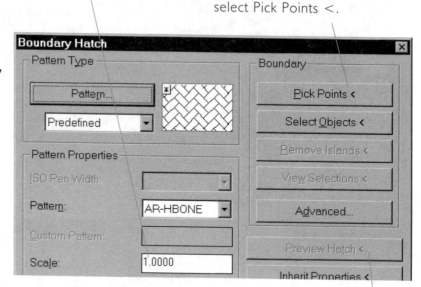

Boundary Hatch

Pattern Type
Pattern...
Predefined

Pattern Properties
ISO Pen Width:
Pattern: AR-HBONE
Custom Pattern:
Scale: 1.0000

Boundary
Pick Points <
Select Objects <
Remove Islands <
View Selections <
Advanced...
Preview Hatch <
Inherit Properties <

7 Pick here. The boundary around the point you pick will be highlighted. Press Enter.

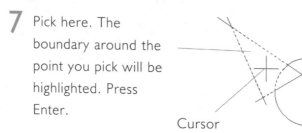

Cursor

HANDY TIP **At step 9 you could return to the dialogue box and change the scale setting to see the effect.**

8 The Boundary Hatch dialogue box returns. Click on Preview Hatch <.

9 If you are happy with the preview at this point, click on Continue.

10 The Boundary Hatch dialogue box reappears. Click on the Apply button to apply the pattern to the drawing.

Hatch Patterns and Content Explorer

The Content Explorer can be used to drag hatch patterns into a drawing (see page 119 for an explanation of the Content Explorer). To drag a hatch pattern into the drawing, follow the steps below.

1 Click on the Hatch tab.

HANDY TIP

Before dragging a hatch pattern onto a drawing, double-click on it to check its properties.

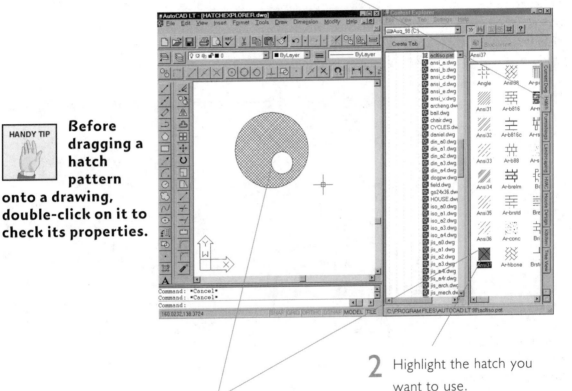

2 Highlight the hatch you want to use.

3 Drag it into the drawing.

If you double-click on the hatch pattern in the Content Explorer, the Boundary Hatch dialogue box will appear. You may then choose the settings you want.

If you look under the Setting menus on the Explorer, you will see that settings for hatch patterns can also be preset.

Text Styles

AutoCAD LT comes with a STANDARD text style. You can define your own styles and use them while inserting text into the drawing or a part of the dimensioning style.

Here are the steps for creating a style called EXTERIOR:

1 From the Format drop-down menu select Text Style... The Text Style dialogue box appears. You define the style you want in this box.

2 Click on New.

Standard AutoCAD LT style

The font the style is based on

Select Arial

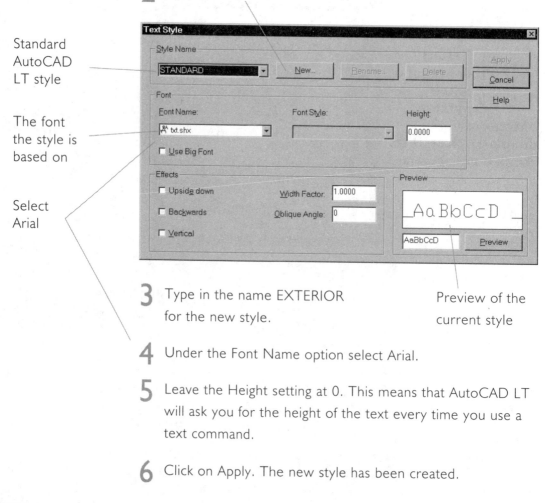

Preview of the current style

3 Type in the name EXTERIOR for the new style.

4 Under the Font Name option select Arial.

5 Leave the Height setting at 0. This means that AutoCAD LT will ask you for the height of the text every time you use a text command.

6 Click on Apply. The new style has been created.

Using a New Style

The new style EXTERIOR created on the previous page will now be offered as an option in any command that uses text styles.

Try the following:

1 From the Dimension drop-down menu select Style...

2 In the Dimension Style dialogue box click on Annotation. In the annotation dialogue box the style EXTERIOR is listed under styles.

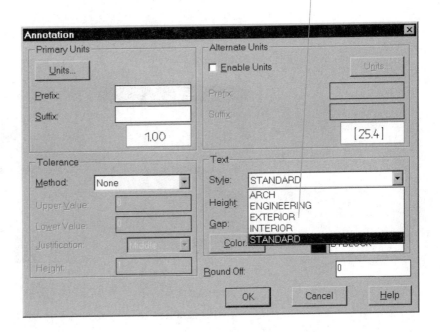

3 When the style is selected it can be used as the style for the dimension text.

Similarly, if you run the mtext command the EXTERIOR style will appear under the properties tab, allowing you to use it as a text style.

Viewports

When you are creating a drawing in AutoCAD LT you are working in model space. Model space initially gives you a single view of a drawing. You can view the drawing in several different ways if you divide up the model space screen into several viewports. To do this:

1 Open a drawing in the usual way. Try opening the 'forest' drawing in the Samples folder. It will open into a single view in model space.

2 From the View drop-down menu select Tiled Viewports.

Shows viewport arrangement visually

Returns you to a single viewport

Preset arrangements

A saved arrangement can be restored

You may delete an existing saved arrangement

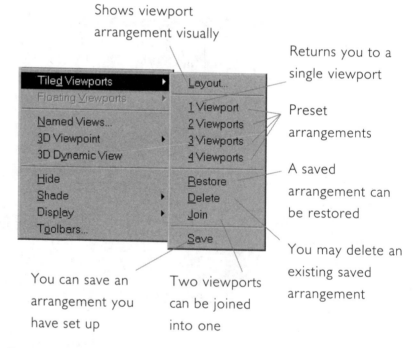

You can save an arrangement you have set up

Two viewports can be joined into one

3 Click on the Layout... option. The screen opposite is displayed.

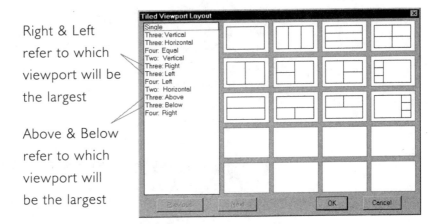

Right & Left
refer to which
viewport will be
the largest

Above & Below
refer to which
viewport will
be the largest

4 Select 'Three: Left'. Your screen will divide into three tiled viewports, each one showing the same view of the drawing.

5 Move the cross-hairs from one viewport to another and the cross-hairs will change to an arrow. The active or current viewport is the one with the cross-hairs. To make another viewport active just click in it.

You cannot have a different drawing in each viewport.

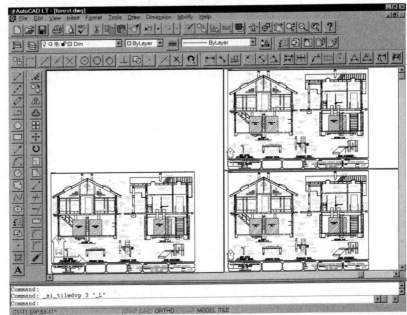

6 When a viewport is active you can draw and edit in it in the normal way.

7 Each viewport can have a different setting for the zoom level, grid and snap. The image below shows three different levels of zoom.

REMEMBER

You can start a command in one tiled viewport and finish it in another.

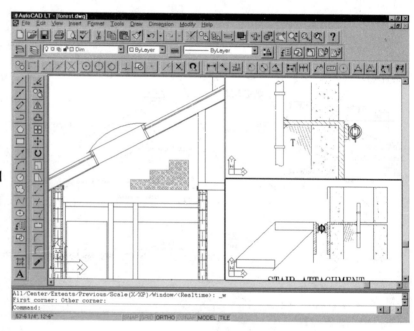

8 A command can be started in one viewport and continued in another. Try drawing a line from one to another. Remember that you start the command in an active viewport and when you move to the inactive port you must click first to make it active.

9 To return to a single viewport, select the View drop-down menu, then Tiled Viewports and finally I Viewport. The view that appears in the single port is the current or active one.

Saving and Restoring Tiled Viewports

Once the viewports are arranged suitably you can save the configuration. This will allow you to return to the same arrangement any time the drawing is opened. The restore option allows you to restore a pre-saved arrangement.

To save an arrangement, follow these steps:

Saving and restoring viewports can speed up work on large, complex drawings.

1 Set up an arrangement of tiled viewports.

2 From the View drop-down menu select Tiled Viewports.

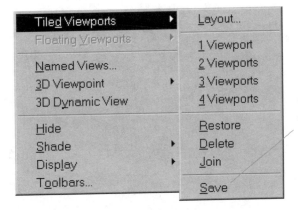

3 Click on Save.

4 The command line prompts '?/Name for new viewport configuration:'. Type in a name and press Enter.

Now return to a single viewport and test the saved arrangement by restoring it as follows:

1 From the View drop-down menu select Tiled Viewports and then Restore.

2 In response to the command line prompt '?/Name the configuration to restore:' type in its name and press Enter. If you cannot remember its names type the '?' and press Enter twice.

The View Command

The view command allows you to save a particular view of the drawing. You may save a view and restore it at a later stage. For example, a saved view can be accessed during the plot command. Here are the steps to create a view and then restore it:

HANDY TIP

Saving and restoring a view can speed up work on large complex drawings.

1 Zoom to see the complete drawing.

2 At the command line type 'view' and press Enter. The following options are displayed '?/Delete/Restore/Save/Window:'. Type 'w' for windows and press Enter.

3 Type in a name for the view and press Enter.

4 In response to 'First window, Other window' pick two points to define the view.

To see the view you saved, try the following:

1 Type view and press Enter. From the options select 'r' for restore.

2 In response to 'View name to restore:' type in the view name and press Enter or type '?' and press Enter twice to see a list of stored views.

HANDY TIP

Save a view of an area of the drawing you want to plot separately.

You can also see a list of saved views under the Named Views... option on the Views drop-down menu.

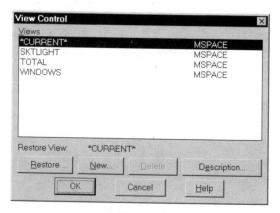

The Plotting Procedure

A drawing can be plotted/printed at any scale. You can also ask AutoCAD LT to 'fit' a drawing on any sheet size, regardless of whether it is an A4 or Ao or larger size.

The Print / Plot command is found on the File drop-down menu. You can also type plot at the command line. The Print / Plot dialogue box is quite complex. Only some of the options can be treated in this text. The steps involved in printing a drawing are:

HANDY TIP
You can change the electronic paper size even when you have finished the drawing.

1 Select the printer/plotter the drawing will be printed on. If you have several printers/plotters, this is an important step because it can determine the size of the paper you can use. AutoCAD LT will not allow you to plot to a sheet size larger than what your printer can take.

2 Decide on the size of the paper you will print on.

3 Decide on the scale of the plot. If you set the electronic sheet before you started drawing to a multiple of the standard paper sizes (A1, A2, A3, etc) then this will be easy.

4 Decide whether you want to print to the Drawing Limits/ Extents/Display or a Saved View. Limits is out to the size of the electronic paper size; Extents is out to the very edge of the actual drawing; Display is what you can see on the screen before you issue the plot command; View allows you to select pre-saved views (see the View command).

5 Preview the plot to see that it works OK. This is an essential step. It can save you both a considerable amount of time and paper.

6 Plot the drawing.

Plotting the Work

Issue the print command: File>Print... The Print / Plot Configuration dialogue box appears.

1 Click here and choose your printer.

2 Click here to select the drawing units and the sheet size.

3 Click on Display to print what you have on the screen.

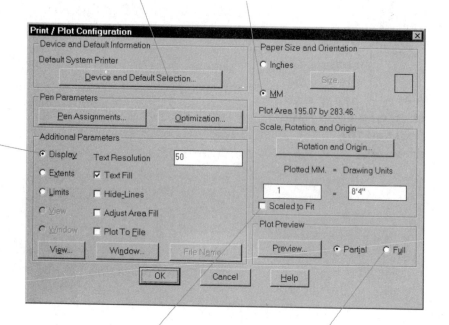

4 Place a tick in 'Scaled to Fit' and AutoCAD LT will select a plot scale for you to fit the drawing on the selected paper size.

5 Select Full and click on the Preview button to see what the drawing will plot like using the parameters you just defined.

6 After viewing the preview, you might decide to rotate the drawing by 90 degrees. To do so press Esc or Enter to leave the preview and click on the Rotation and Origin button.

...cont'd

Check the electronic paper size you set up initially. Use it to work out a plot scale.

7 Click to rotate the drawing. Then try the Full Preview option again.

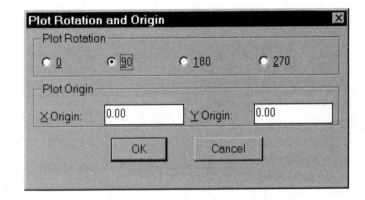

If you are lost for a scale try plot to 'fit'. See what calculation AutoCAD LT makes and then round it off.

8 When you are satisfied with the preview click on OK in the Print / Plot Configuration dialogue box.

Printing problems?

Many problems associated with printing are due to either not having a plotter set up correctly or not having the electronic drawing page set up correctly. These are two areas you should look at carefully if you cannot manage to print drawings at the correct scale. The example given here forced the drawing to fit on a sheet of paper. To plot to a specific scale, the scale must be entered in the Print / Plot Configuration dialogue box.

A plot to fit scale of 283.464 to 25002 can be rounded off to a 1:100 plot scale.

If you usually work with A3 pages with drawings at 1:100, then it is a good idea to set up your electronic page at 100 times the size of the A3 page. When you need to plot on A3 paper the drawing must be reduced by 100 times. This method saves time.

Plotting Line Thicknesses

Lines created using any drawing command other than the polyline or donut are described by AutoCAD LT as having a line thickness of 0. This in effect means that they will have the thickness of the pen that is used to plot them. Architectural and engineering drawings are printed in black and white traditionally, with line thicknesses or weights being used to emphasise features in the drawing. To simulate this line weight effect in AutoCAD LT you can apply a line thickness to a colour.

Colours are usually assigned to layers. Think of colours as pen thicknesses when setting up the layers.

To do this select the Pen Assignments button on the Print / Plot Configuration dialogue box. In the Pen Assignments dialogue box that opens you can assign a thickness to each colour. In the illustration below, the colour red (pen 1) has a thickness of 0.3mm applied to it, while the colour yellow (pen 2) is assigned 0.5mm thickness.

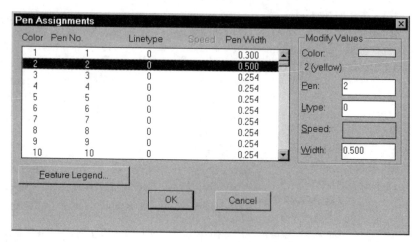

When plotting the drawing on a traditional pen plotter, place a 0.3 pen in pen location 1 (where colour red was), etc. The more recent bubble/ink jet plotters or thermal plotters will understand what you want once they are set to monochrome.

Happy drawing and plotting!

Index